Praise for
Breaking the Coaching Code

I0069894

Breaking the Coaching Code is an incredibly uplifting and affirming text for coaches, reconnecting the reader with the heart and soul of coaching. Karen Foy shines a light on what makes us human and how, as coaches, this is the essence of the value we bring to our clients.

Professor Rebecca Jones, Professor in Coaching and Behavioural Change, Henley Business School

This book provides an important provocation for any coach seeking to develop their practice. While accepting that all coaches need to know the foundations of our craft, Karen Foy reminds us that ultimately, we will need to face ourselves and take responsibility for the way we work. We need to question what we have been taught, break the rules (or at least some of them) and find our own way. This book provides some practical ideas and useful reflections to help coaches take the next steps on this journey. It is compelling and inspiring, with a wealth of references and perspectives for further reading. It is a 'must-have' on any coach's bookshelf.

Laurence Barrett, author of *A Jungian Approach to Coaching: The Theory and Practice of Turning Leaders into People*, and visiting faculty at INSEAD, Henley Business School and the Cambridge Institute of Continuing Education

This book captures what makes coaching so powerful: a warm space where you feel safe, seen and gently encouraged, with quiet wisdom, to rest and reflect. Karen's narrative is gentle, witty and sprinkled with a touch of pixie dust. Reading it feels as though it was written with you in mind.

Lorenzo Todorow di San Giorgio, Head of Executive Coaching & Faculty Member, University College London School of Management Global MBA

Karen has achieved something quite special with this book. It is a beautiful read. *Breaking the Coaching Code* gives those of us entering the second half of life as a coach something really meaningful to reflect on. Karen truly demonstrates the art of partnership in the way this book is written, taking a number of key coaching themes and dilemmas all of us ponder on as coaches, offering something of herself and her own journey, and then asking you to consider the same. Karen encourages us all to think beyond the coaching competencies and to consider how we really show up as coaches, beautifully describing the art of coaching and its sometimes challenging juxtaposition with the science of coaching. I can't recommend it enough.

Sarah Leach MSc, PCC, Executive Coach, Coach Educator, Facilitator & Author

Karen's unassuming voice captures the soul of coaching. Humanity and humility shine through her being as she walks alongside us in service of our global profession and artful practice. To move into coaching beyond that which is formulaic or coded into AI, sit with the nuggets of steadfast wisdom generously shared. This is unbound coaching, future-fit for human and system complexity.

Kirsty Knowles, Founder/Owner of Think Being®, ICF & EMCC Coach, Facilitator, Coach Educator, Mentor Coach, Consultant Director of Professional Development & Board Member UK ICF

The book masterfully weaves radical honesty, humour and deep insight to reveal how embracing our humanity is the gateway to truly impactful coaching.

Ana-Maria Chirila, Notary Public, MSc, Certified Executive Coach, UKICF Board Member

Through a combination of stories, honesty and examples, Karen breaks open the coaching code. She challenges us all to move beyond rigid rules and techniques towards radical honesty and genuine connection with the humans we work with. This is a must read for coaches at any stage in their career.

Claire Pedrick MCC, Author, *Simplifying Coaching*

In a profession increasingly filled with expert advice and top tips, Karen Foy's book is a welcome breath of fresh air. A masterful blend of humility and wisdom, and a gentle guide to all of us imperfect humans in our journey to being better able to support other human beings with the challenges they bring to coaching.

Aboodi Shabi PCC, Lecturer in Coaching and Behaviour Change, Henley Business School

Breaking the Coaching Code is not just about coaching; it is about who we are as coaches. With warmth and wisdom, Karen Foy invites us to look beyond technique and into the deeper layers of our presence: our inherited patterns, unspoken expectations and the ways we unconsciously shape the coaching space. This is not about breaking rules for the sake of it; it is about liberation, about stepping into coaching with more of ourselves.

This book speaks to those who are ready to move beyond performative coaching and into a deeper, more conscious way of working. Karen weaves together theory with her own journey of discovery, offering stories, insights and reflective practices that invite us to hold our knowledge lightly and trust in who we are becoming. Karen argues that coaching is not just about what we say or do; it is about the space we create through our presence, our attention and our willingness to meet ourselves fully in the work. Who we are being as a coach is our most powerful tool and Karen calls us to examine this with honesty and courage.

Karen encourages us to reflect on how we show up in the coaching relationship, how we hold the tension between knowing and not knowing, between structure and flow. This is a book for those willing to embrace the discomfort of self-discovery, those ready to bring their whole, human selves into their coaching practice. If you are curious about how your way of being influences how you coach and if you are prepared to step into a journey that transforms not only your clients but also yourself, then this book will be a generous and wise companion on that path.

Dr Eunice Aquilina, founder of eaconsult and author of *Embodying Authenticity* (2016) and *Stepping into Your Power* (2021)

Breaking
the Coaching Code

How great
coaches
transcend
the rules

Karen Foy

First published in Great Britain by Practical Inspiration Publishing, 2025

© Karen Foy, 2025

The moral rights of the author have been asserted.

ISBN   9781788608282   (paperback)
       9781788608275   (hardback)
       9781788608299   (ebook)

All rights reserved. This book, or any portion thereof, may not be reproduced without the express written permission of the publisher.

Every effort has been made to trace copyright holders and to obtain their permission for the use of copyright material. The publisher apologizes for any errors or omissions and would be grateful if notified of any corrections that should be incorporated in future reprints or editions of this book.

EU GPSR representative: LOGOS EUROPE, 9 rue Nicolas Poussin, LA ROCHELLE 17000, France Contact@logoseurope.eu

Want to bulk-buy copies of this book for your team and colleagues? We can customize the content and co-brand *Breaking The Coaching Code* to suit your business's needs.

Please email info@practicalinspiration.com for more details.

Practical Inspiration Publishing

All the world is made of faith, and trust, and pixie dust.

Peter Pan

Thank you to all the people I have worked and played with over the years for guiding me back to my own power through their faith and trust in me, especially my husband, Tommy, for being my never-ending supply of pixie dust.

Contents

Foreword...xi

Part 1: Radical self-honesty

Introduction: singing the chorus 3

1   Reasons for transcending the rules.................7

2   Exploring your personal agenda 15

3   Dropping the performance 27

4   The myth of the objective observer..............39

5   The implications for presence
    and mindset 49

Part 2: Curious acceptance of difference

6   Building a brave space for exploration 59

7   Birdwatching for coaches 67

8   Fearing the unknown.......................................73

Part 3: The pathway to co-creation

9   Transcending the rules in practice................ 81

10 Getting to the heart of the matter................ 85

11 Following the thread.......................................97

12 Coaching the person, not the task...............105

13 Listening with purpose 109

**14 If you are not evoking awareness, you
     might as well give up** 121

15 Not everyone is looking for action...............129

**16 Developing professional and ethical
     maturity** 139

17 The end of the beginning..............................145

References... 151

About the author 157

Index..159

Foreword

Learning to be a coach is a journey of discovery, a lifelong vocation. The situations we encounter, the people we meet, the knowledge we acquire, the experiences we reflect upon – all come together to influence how we are as coaches.

Although that journey of discovery is long and sometimes challenging, it need not be one that we take in isolation as a solo traveller. The current generation of coaches benefits hugely from those who are themselves already further along the journey. And we benefit even more when those in the vanguard choose to enrich our coaching practice by sharing their reflections with us.

Just occasionally in life, we are lucky to meet one of those trail-blazers and to recognize that their wisdom, authority and expertise shines especially brightly. When that person also possesses the rare ability to be able to pass on their knowledge and experience with warmth, relevance and humility, then we are doubly lucky.

As you will quickly discover in the pages that follow, Karen Foy is one such person.

Over the past decade, a new generation of coaches have benefited beyond measure by being trained by Karen at

Henley Business School – me included. In the classroom, Karen has the knack of finding the right words and the right stories to answer the many difficult questions that are chewed over every day by both novice and experienced coaches. She also has an unerring ability to ask the right question in the first place.

This book highlights and discusses some of the uncertainties about coaching that many of us will have pondered over the years. It's all about how we are as coaches: our humanity, our curiosity, our authenticity and our integrity. But it's about more than that because it's infused with Karen's unique savviness, or as she herself might say, it's also about how we can make the coaching magic happen.

This is a book about being comfortable with uncertainty in the pursuit of possibility. It's about knowing the rules, but it's also about breaking the rules.

Karen follows in a long line of skilled practitioners who understand that there are times when stepping outside the conventional way of doing things can help spark that magic. Pablo Picasso advised those who wanted to emulate his creative success to 'learn the rules like a pro, so you can break them like an artist', while the Dalai Lama told his followers to 'know the rules well, so you can break them effectively'.

Karen's work exemplifies this way of being. Her thinking is firmly rooted in an acute understanding of research-based scientific coaching practice. She knows what works – and what doesn't – and she can tell us why that's the case. Some coaches will be content only ever to operate in this zone. However, Karen offers us the opportunity to travel to a new paradigm. In these pages, she takes us beyond mere academic theory by adding a layer of pragmatism and practicality born out of many years operating beyond the classroom in real-life coaching situations. She helps us to recognize that our coaching can reach this higher level when we are prepared to think and behave differently. She argues persuasively that it is at this point that new truths and insights are uncovered.

There are so many scenarios where we as coaches could all benefit from having a distilled version of Karen Foy's wisdom neatly packaged up in our pockets, ready to call upon when we are uncertain or in need of guidance. There is no doubt that this book fulfils that functional need. But perhaps it also operates at a higher level too by helping us to unlock a few more moments of magic on our lifelong journey of coaching discovery. And who would argue against the benefits of more magic in the lives of coaches and in the lives of the people we coach?

Dr Darren Henley CBE, Chief
Executive of Arts Council England

Part 1

Radical self-honesty

Introduction

singing the chorus

I remember going on a holiday with my adult sister and her husband when I was about nine or ten. We were on a campsite on the east coast of Yorkshire and there was a clubhouse with a talent show. I nagged my brother-in-law to put my name down as a competitor. I was planning to sing 'The clapping song', popular at the time. Yes, I am that old. I am still not sure if he did add my name to the list or just pretended, but the moment I thought I was on the list the reality hit – I only knew the chorus, and I couldn't really sing.

That experience and the panic that I felt in that clubhouse resurfaced the moment I committed to writing this book. For years I have loved sharing my learning with new coaches and supporting them to grow into their craft, and for years I promised myself I would capture all the learning in a book. But suddenly I felt I only knew the chorus and others could sing better. It was only with the encouragement of colleagues and the coaches I have worked with that I found the courage to share a little of the wisdom I have picked up along the way.

What I realized as I started to write is that I cannot claim the credit for whatever nuggets I share with you, because they represent the collective wisdom of all the people I have met along the way. Everyone I have coached, every teacher, mentor and supervisor, and all the wise colleagues I have had the great fortune of working with or just speaking with. I heard somewhere that you become the company you keep, and I have had the great good fortune of being in the company of so many wise and generous people. As I worked through each stage of the book, I struggled to remember if what I was saying came from me or was created in a conversation between me and another coach, and much of the time I wasn't sure. I guess what I want to encourage you to do is find great mentors, supervisors and experienced coaches who can help you to grow into the best coach you can be.

I don't offer any universal truths about coaching in this book; I merely offer my truth as it stands today. Who knows what it will be this time next year, because the profession and me are learning all the time. But I did want to rustle up some courage to share what I know now because for the last 10 years or so my focus has been on developing the next generation of coaches. Just walking a small part of the road to becoming a coach with so many fabulous people has been a privilege.

My aim is always to remind everyone that self-discovery is the first step to becoming a great coach. The deeper you are willing to dig to accept all the kaleidoscope parts of yourself, the more right you have to witness another person in that vulnerable state.

We all have a unique gift to add to the coaching community, and it is probably something to do with whatever we are currently masking or hiding from the world. We all have parts of our personality that we have decided are wrong or too different to share with the world, so we try not to show them. This book offers you opportunities to uncover that uniqueness. Coaching is all about choice, and the choice is yours – in this book, there are prompts throughout the text for you to use if you find them useful. Remember, I am not the expert, and I have no desire to be. I am a fellow traveller who may or may not be a little further down the road, but I only know some things because of all the wrong turnings I have taken. So, enjoy the road, wherever it takes you.

1

Reasons for transcending the rules

As novices they learn the rules, as intermediates they break the rules, as masters they change the rules and as artisans they transcend the rules.

David Drake (2011, p. 143)

What brought you to a book about breaking the rules? You may be a new coach still proudly clutching your certificate or badge and wanting to learn everything you can about coaching. Or maybe you have been coaching for a while and have got a little stuck and want to know how to excel. You could just be rebelling and want to coach in your own sweet way without recourse to widely accepted skills, competencies and processes. My hope is that this exploration of the generally accepted coaching codes and reflections on how the rules can be transcended will inspire you to develop your own unique coaching approach.

My drive to support the next generation of coaches connects to an ongoing theme for me: finding shortcuts. When I started this book, I wanted to help others get to a level of skill in coaching that had taken me over 20 years to achieve. I was convinced that if I could download all that I and others had learnt from our decades of practice, I could save coaches a lot of time and trouble. What was the point of working in this field for so long if it wasn't to gather and share insights?

My plan was to work through all the pitfalls for developing coaches I and other coach educators, mentors and supervisors had observed, then offer my solutions for how those could be avoided. But it quickly became clear I was setting myself up as just another 'expert' telling everyone I have the Holy Grail. I wondered, how could I be in service of my fellow coaches and point a finger to something useful without it needing to be 'the truth'?

Gradually, through reading, conversations and reflection, I realized that on the journey to growing as a coach, there is a clear place for learning the fundamentals of the process and understanding the rules and practices. But alongside this development of skills, the *doing* of coaching, there is an inward journey to *being* a coach that calls for a willingness to go to the 'scary places', to meet your own 'uglies' and welcome them as an integral part of yourself, and this may be your greatest asset in your unique approach to life and coaching. The rules are just the starting point: the magic happens when you discover how to purposefully break or bend them to suit the needs of the people you work with.

Carl Jung popularized the idea of the two halves of life. The first is spent building our identity and ego, what we show to the world; the second is where we realize there is more to us, a deeper purpose. In his book *Falling Upward*, Richard Rohr (2012) asserts that between the two halves is often a 'fall'. The first half of life focuses on success, working harder, getting better, achieving more, following the rules. This is great and reaps rewards – until it doesn't. And that's often after a fall, a redundancy, an illness, a loss of some sort or, less dramatically, that sense of 'Is this it? Is this all there is?' To embrace this 'fall' and stay with it in the discomfort until it teaches us the lesson we need to learn is the work of the second half of life. Leaning into and allowing that discomfort to teach us brings us to the place that, for decades, may have seemed elusive: acceptance and connection to one's own internal wisdom. This is where we transcend the rules and connect with our own wisdom and purpose.

This post-fall second half of life rings so true with me in the sense that it is not just about getting older. I am sure we can all think of examples of people who have gained years but seem to have missed the wisdom distribution. Age does not equal wisdom; we must learn from our experiences to gain it. In the same way in coaching, the number of hours we have coached is no guarantee of quality. We may have thousands of hours of experience, or we may have had the same experience thousands of times. I have known young people with the wisdom of elders and new coaches who demonstrate masterful coaching from the beginning. Coaches learn their skills and hone their craft towards an external marker of 'good enough', and many of them become stuck at the crossing point between first- and second-half thinking. What keeps them stuck, and what can free them?

How might coaches experience the 'fall'?

What is the fall that holds the bridge to the wisdom of the second half in the coaching profession? It is my assertion that the fall that is developing for the coaching profession lies in the growth of artificial intelligence (AI). As the coaching industry continues to expand with the introduction of AI and coaching platforms offering low-cost services, coaches will need to offer something extra in order to survive and thrive. Life and work are becoming increasingly complex, uncertain and challenging for many of us. Anecdotally, I notice leaders seeking coaching to help them navigate the ambiguity of life and, like the rest of us, seek a purposeful one. Maybe this is something that will be gradually programmed into future iterations of AI, but it is not there yet. Can a computer program deal with ambiguity, get a felt sense of the unexpressed pain a human is experiencing or empathize with a shared human condition? As Dr Holly Andrews, a friend and colleague of mine, has observed in her work exploring psychopathy and coaching, psychopaths are good at mimicking empathy without feeling it, and a coaching bot might be programmed to give the appearance of empathy in much the same way. This means there is no shared felt sense of experience.

I am hardly an expert in the power of AI, as I often rely on children and grandchildren to help me navigate my smartphone. Nonetheless, I understand that while AI programs are constantly learning, essentially they are based on the limitations of the creators of the original input. I was once briefly involved in giving feedback on a program designed to provide pseudo mentoring for an International Coaching Federation credential based on coaching competencies. There were some fundamental differences between my interpretation of certain competencies and the program's understanding of them. When I discussed this with the designer, the explanation was that the algorithm was built from the interpretations of coach researchers from another culture to mine. So, who builds the AI? Which interpretations can a coach lean on?

I am sure bigger brains than mine will navigate these nuances eventually, but I remain unconvinced that the messiness of humanity can be coded and replicated so easily. Whenever I have reached out to a coach or a coach supervisor, I have needed to know they can hear, see and feel me from the perspective of sharing my humanity and imperfections. Before I share vulnerabilities, shame and failure, I want to know that they have experienced those emotions and can recognize how powerful they are. Coaches will need to transcend the rules and draw on their full humanity to meet this need and differentiate themselves in a crowded space. Many coaches stuck in the first stage of coaching will lose their custom to the easy access of coaching bots or lower-cost platforms, which are getting great satisfaction ratings according to the CoachHub platform. So, business share might be one fall we face as coaches, but what about the more personal falls?

As coaches, we can all face a personal fall. My fall came years into my coaching. I was doing a good job, I was learning lots, gathering qualifications tools and techniques along with clients. I was even making little excursions into the scary places, but always with a guiding thread bringing me safely back out of the labyrinth. Of course, I had my personal insights and reflected on my own failings regularly, and I compared myself to others who could do this thing called coaching better. And on good days, I even marked myself up a bit and got arrogant about my ability. But there was still so much of me on that 'Am I good? Am I rubbish?' see-saw that the answer to each of those questions resulted in me putting more work into my performance and then seeking external approval to validate myself.

I was set on the pathway to my fall by an assessment when I was working as an associate. The feedback suggested that I may not be strong or challenging enough to work with the 'big boys', the people in powerful jobs. I was being measured against one view of what effective executive coaching was, and I was found to be wanting. As I looked at all the highly vocal and opinionated coaches around me who, on the surface, displayed no lack of belief in themselves or their powers, I knew I didn't fit the mould, and for some reason, at that moment, in that space, it felt like I was falling into the deep. I can hardly connect with that feeling from my vantage point now, 10 or so years later, but I do remember the dark roads I went down.

I spent time trying the things that had helped me up to that point – the first-half-of-life stuff, like working harder and conforming more. But that merely confirmed the fact that I wasn't that person, that I was wrong. This was my real fall – not thinking that I did something wrong but thinking that I *am* wrong. Any deep and honest self-reflection can feel like a dark and lonely place. It is not easy to sit alone and challenge yourself to grow without trying to numb or defend. Gloria Steinem's book captures the experience in the title: *The Truth Will Set You Free, But First It Will Piss You Off!* Unless we do this deep work, we cannot hope to sit alongside anyone else as they face their own dragons and not try to rescue them. Even more importantly, we have no right to expect anyone to allow us to witness them fighting their dragons when our own are blowing smoke behind us, clouding our view.

This part of our journey to being our best self as a coach is not quick or easy, and no one in the world can give you the map. It's your labyrinth. Only you know its twists and turns. But the reward is finding that the cracks you are trying to conceal are likely to be the doorway to your unique gift as a coach and a human. This is the real work to get to the second half of a coaching life. It includes lots of reflection and supervision, and the first part of this book aims to set you on the journey to places you might want to explore. The work is never finished, but as you emerge from the labyrinth with a renewed purpose, you can honour the rules of the first half of your coaching life and transcend them to become the best version of you.

All these years later, after all the work and the tears, I can truly thank the harsh and painful 'truth' I received for helping me to discover and accept that I don't fit that particular mould, but my coaching is perfect in all its imperfections for the people who need a coach like me – a coach who can witness your pain without rushing to the rescue, who can hold your self-belief for you until you are ready to take ownership of it, who can afflict your comfort with compassion and strength when you want to move away from the dark, who celebrates you for your courage to trust your hard-won wisdom in full and walks home with you to all that you are. What was the road to this? Radical acceptance brought about by self-awareness. This enables us to trust that we know deeply who we are and what that means for our coaching, and to be willing to critically explore the rules and accepted truths of this profession of ours to find our own voices in the noise.

If you are willing to challenge yourself to move away from the shoreline of trusted techniques, tools and approaches, then maybe you are ready to grow into your own personal brand of wisdom and coaching that allows you to *be* a coach rather than *do* coaching. In this book, I guide you through some of the core coaching skills and offer a second-half-of-coaching-life view, showing you some of the paths less trodden and inviting you to stop along the way to reflect on some of the barriers that may have prevented you from walking them before now. My only aim for you is the same one I have for every client or coach I work with, and that is to remind you who you truly are as a coach and to help you accept that you do not have to be a perfect coach to be a transformational presence and that often your own brand of human frailty is exactly what the world needs right now – grown-up coaches who can respect the rules but not be bound by them.

2

Exploring your personal agenda

Please don't try to help me. I mean it's very kind of you to want to help people but please don't make it your sole creative motive, because we will feel the weight of your heavy intention, and it will put a strain in our souls.

Elizabeth Gilbert (2015, p. 98)

So, why are you coaching? As a coach educator of many years, the answer I hear more than any other is 'I want to help people'. I am sure this or some version of it is what brings many of us into this line of work, but I am also sure there is something much more compelling and different for each of us. There will be some form of kickback or benefit we are getting that is a much stronger and deeper force at work in the shadows. This is not wrong or shameful, but we should be aware of it. Awareness of our own deeper motivations can really help us to grow up in our coaching. Without exploration, these drivers can have an impact on our behaviour in the coaching conversation, creating a barrier to us doing our best work and potentially affecting our well-being and professionalism.

Marie Adams reflected on a similar question regarding her work as a therapist and gave an important distinction in

The Myth of the Untroubled Therapist. She recognized that the *reason* she had undergone therapist training was different to the *catalyst* (Adams, 2024, p. 88). Your own catalyst may have been experiencing the power of coaching personally and wanting to train to offer that out to others; on the other hand, the motivation could be a far deeper need to 'heal' in others what you have experienced personally. In executive coaching, there are many leaders who have had successful careers and want to continue to make a contribution as a coach to the leaders following after them. It is the same in many other niches, such as women who, after having children, have made successful careers coaching new mothers, and people who have faced challenges relating to diversity and exclusion making careers to help others facing similar challenges. We all have valuable experience that can be a catalyst for getting into the work, and yet the shadow of our unrecognized motivator or reason can loom large.

To throw some light on the shadow, we need a little reflection to illuminate what we are seeking when we coach others. Some of us may be compulsive caregivers; others may need to feel useful, add value or be relevant. We can often discern our particular shade of shadow by reflecting on what gives us pleasure and pain in our coaching. Maybe it's the pleasure we experience when we see our clients get to the 'aha' moment or the dread we experience when we imagine a client giving us negative feedback, or that one pattern we notice about ourselves that we know is unhelpful in our coaching but which we cannot seem to replace with something more useful. In her book, Adams refers to Carl Rogers' admission that working with clients 'provided him with an intimacy he sometimes found difficult in his personal life' (2024, p. 90).

In my own coaching I have always been committed to the concept of walking people home to their true self, their own wisdom. I fully adhere to the humanistic perspective that, as Jane Austen (1814, p. 257) wrote in *Mansfield Park*: 'We have all a better guide in ourselves, if we would attend to it, than any other person can be.'

I find this approach stops me from trying to be an expert in someone else's life and keeps me fully focused on them claiming their own power. But, for many years, the irony was lost on me that this was my quest in my own life: to find self-acceptance and to know and trust that, in the words of Billy Joel, 'I love you just the way you are', I was working so hard in coaching to get the other person to love and accept me that often unconsciously, I might have colluded with them or not offered a perspective that could challenge their world-view or challenge their place of comfort, all in service of staying liked and appreciated. I only became fully aware after reflecting on the question 'Why do I coach?' and not letting myself off the hook regarding the catalyst for my choice.

This catalyst resulted in me once being described as everyone's favourite aunt. Although this was offered as constructive feedback, it felt like an insult. However, the truth was that I was doing too much to care for the people I was coaching. In my early days as a coach, this translated into me taking far too much responsibility for my clients, taking notes on actions, sending long emails after sessions and working hard to help them find solutions to their enquiries – all really unhelpful behaviours. Spending time working through the experiences that led to those beliefs and behaviours meant

I could hold clearer boundaries in my coaching and leave responsibilities where they belonged: with the person whose life it was.

Another example is the coach who is so invested in adding value within a coaching relationship that they present the persona of being the cleverest person in the room. Imagine that, as a coach, you are working with a leader and you feel you need to add value. You have worked together a few times and all is going well, but now they have come up against a tricky situation and seem stuck about where to go or what to do. How might your driver to add value impact your work? Maybe you don't know what you would do if you were in that situation, or maybe you do – I'm not sure which would be worse for you and your client. I am guessing there is at least a chance that if you have some knowledge, from your past experience, that might be useful about what might work, you might start to think you can 'take off your coaching hat' for just a minute to offer your thoughts and ideas. Maybe the leader likes those ideas so you take a breath, relax and feel the relief of being back on solid ground. You can justify your slip into mentoring some other time – for now, all is good as you have added value.

Sadly, these and other motivators will keep us locked in the first half of our coaching lives, never transcending the threshold to add real value and power to our coaching. As coaches, we need to reflect radically and honestly on what we personally are seeking in our coaching and push past the BS that tells us, no, we really are only there to support and help others. A concept often shared in mental health work is that unhealed people hear with their triggers, not their ears.

Until we have examined our motivations and transformed them into something that we are aware of, we will continue to project our needs onto the people we work with.

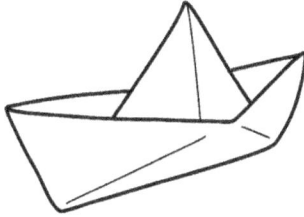

Robin Shohet, a pioneering supervisor of coaches and therapists, shared a story on a recent coaching supervision programme we were both facilitating that encapsulates the state of mind we are working towards as coaches. He talked about the 'empty boat'. Consider you are on a lake or sailing out of a harbour and your boat bumps into another. It's likely that you will face the wrath of the other sailor for your incompetence and the damage you caused. This is a justifiable reaction – you were in charge and steered into the other vessel. Now imagine you are no longer sailing that boat; it is empty and drifting. It is still heading for the other unlucky sailor and bumps into their vessel, causing the same damage. Who can the sailor shout at now?

Our aim in coaching from a second-half-of-coaching-life perspective is to become an empty boat, free of drivers and triggers. If we have loaded our boat up with all our needs (to add value, to be loved, to be respected), then there are lots of triggers for us to react to. What does 'being triggered' feel like? Try this on for a minute or two and reflect on the question:

> What is the worst feedback your client could give you? Give your answer here.

There's your trigger, or at least one of them. You will work hard, without even recognizing it, to ensure your clients never say this about you. Let's say your answer was: 'Well, this is not helping at all.' If you are listening with your 'must add value' trigger, what might your response be? You might shrink down and let your own gremlins in on how rubbish you are as a coach, or you might 'up your game' and start working harder to help more, offering new approaches and tricks, aka coaching tools and techniques, in a frenzied attempt to help. The more fruitful work is to find the place inside where this feared accusation can be accepted. Maybe there are times you are not helpful, don't add value or whatever it is you fear, but the more it is welcomed, the less fearful it becomes. Then you will be able to respond from a place of courage to maybe sit in silence or ask: 'So what would help?'

If you are the empty boat, meaning you are fully aware of the trigger, you have worked through and transformed your relationship with it. Now the trigger is not attached to the detonator. From this perspective, a coach who has moved more into their own wisdom is more likely to move to curiosity, rather than judgement of themselves or the other person, and ask 'So, what could help?' or 'What would be more useful?' They can start to welcome that previously feared feedback and learn from it.

Viewed from a coaching competency perspective, this is the coaching mindset we are aiming for as we progress from our novice state. We are not aiming to ignore our own thoughts, feelings and emotions, but rather to use them more effectively in service of the client. We all know what it can feel like to be lost, stuck or self-critical. Connecting with those experiences can be the basis of our compassion and support for our clients, as it means we can keep the focus on them and not on resolving our past hurts through their work.

As discussed earlier, the motivation for many who are training as a coach is 'to help others' – a problematic objective to say the least. We are all born with the inner light of wisdom within us, and we can often unintentionally deny that wisdom in another person when we think they need us to show them the way. Wanting to help others comes from a loving and compassionate, albeit misguided, place within us. It is not just that it sets a power differential in the relationship from the start – taking this stance creates a whole host of self-inflicted expectations on the coach and encourages the person being coached to take the more passive position. Perhaps a more equitable and realistic approach would be to focus on being useful in the coaching relationship.

Whose monkeys, whose circus?

'Not my circus, not my monkeys' may sound lacking in care, but this was one of the most liberating insights I gained when reflecting on how to develop a coaching mindset – the recognition that I do have a responsibility to my clients, but not for them or their lives. To someone like me, a recovering people pleaser, this took some accepting. Acceptance came when I acknowledged that when I take responsibility for something, I am really saying I don't think you can do this without me. That brought me up short.

It is possible that there are twin beliefs operating in us as coaches when we start to behave as if the session relies heavily on us and what we are bringing to the table. One is that to add value, we have to be seen to be doing something amazing, and the other is that we don't believe the person we are coaching is up to the task of resolving their own dilemmas. Many of us have heard the underpinning belief of coaching that our clients are whole and resourceful, but how many of us truly believe it and operate with that guiding principle?

How often have you felt you have knowledge or experience that you absolutely know the person you are working with can benefit from and that they don't have already? Follow that thought to the end and recognize what that encourages you to do or say, and even further, what that does for the client and their sense of autonomy. It is not surprising that we feel such a strong urge to 'know' – when were any of us ever rewarded for not knowing? A key shift from first- to second-half-of-life coaching is the level of responsibility the coach assumes on behalf of their client.

We know from therapy research (McKenna and Davis, 2009), that 40% of the effectiveness of an intervention is due to external factors. This really helps us to keep our egos in check. External factors are all the things that happen outside of the coaching conversation. We need to remember we may only meet with the person for an hour or two a month, and they have a whole other life outside of that tiny portion of their time. Not only will they have support from their networks, but life changes and evolves, so even the stickiest situations resolve and alter without any obvious change in the client.

The coach can draw on external factors in a session, such as by asking the client to consider their support networks, but the real work is with the client. The most useful insight this can offer coaches focused on getting to that 'aha moment' is that they should stop making the 'aha' their goal and their personal measure of success. It may not happen in the session. A bit like fertilization and pregnancy might happen two days after the act, while the woman is in a supermarket queue, insight and 'aha's may come several days after the conversation has ended, when you are nowhere nearby.

As coaches, we can get attached to our favourite tools or techniques and think they are the magic ingredient that makes our coaching effective. McKenna and Davis' (2009) research highlights this is not likely to be the case, as only 15% of the effectiveness in this study was found to be a result of tools and techniques. Hope accounted for another 15%. This relates to the client's belief that coaching is going to be effective. So just planning and booking coaching may take someone 15% of the way to success. The other major factor in the effectiveness of coaching is the relationship that is created between coach and client, something we will explore in Part 2.

We have a responsibility to do our own work so that we can be at our best with our clients and work with them so that they can decide what they need and want to change and how they want to do it. We do this by listening to them as whole people and evoking awareness to the best of our ability. We are not responsible for their success or otherwise – remember that 40% of that has nothing to do with us.

It can be a life's work transforming our triggers and staying firmly in the role of coach, but awareness is the key. Let's ensure we remain radically honest with ourselves, always reflecting when we are drawn to less useful behaviours by something that happens in the coaching. As O'Hanlon (2019) says: 'You've got to be what you are to get where you are going. If you resist or deny where you are and who you are, it's hard to move on to where you want to be.'

There are some reflection prompts below to help you begin to understand the triggers that lie in wait for you. Rather than writing the first thing that comes to mind, spend some time mulling them over. The more you understand yourself and your triggers, the better you will be as a coach. Sussman (2007) proposes that the development of empathy and compassion comes from personal suffering. If we can face our own history with honesty and compassion, then we can be a better guide for the people we work with. We all have triggers, and there is no shame in that. The greater shame for you, and your clients, is in denying they are there.

My summary reflections

- We all have different reasons and motivators to pursue coaching.
- Awareness of personal drivers and triggers can help manage them.
- Acceptance of imperfections takes the power away from triggers.
- A coach may have a responsibility *to* the client, but not *for* them.

Your reflection prompts

- Why do you coach?

- Now that you know what you fear hearing from your clients (based on your response to the earlier question), what do you notice happening to you if you think they are in danger of saying this?

- How can you begin to transform this trigger in service of your clients?

- What are your signs that you are taking too much responsibility in the partnership?

3

Dropping the performance

Much of what separates the great from the good is deep presence, relaxation of the conscious mind, which allows the unconscious to flow unhindered.... The Grandmaster looks at less and sees more, because his unconscious skill set is much more highly evolved.

(Waitzkin, 2007, pp. 142–143)

A clear difference between first- and second-half-of-life coaching is the level of presence we can bring to the coaching conversation. Operating from beliefs about what a good coach should do in coaching will distract from presence. As my friend and colleague Aboodi Shabi says, 'we must give up the idea of being a good coach to be a great one'. The greatest gift a coach can bring to the coaching relationship is their ability to convey in their whole being that the other person has been fully seen, heard and understood. What a gift! Yet many coaches spend most of their time preparing to perform in the coaching conversation.

Coach training or gaining a credential requires that the coach is constantly evaluated against a set of criteria. No wonder performance looms large. Performing to external standards plus internal drivers to succeed create the perfect conditions for us to be held back from being present. In *Presence-Based Coaching*, Doug Silsbee (2008) defines presence as a state of awareness, a felt experience of timelessness and being connected to a larger truth. This brings us back to 'being' a coach, not necessarily 'doing' coaching. Seeking validation of our own needs and triggers or working hard to follow the 'rules' of coaching will reduce our ability to be present. What does it mean to be present, and what does this look like?

There is a sense of becoming entranced and fascinated by the inner world of the other person. The International Coaching Federation refers to this sensation as the coach becoming a conduit for the other person to have a conversation with themselves. They also talk about the coach 'emptying their head' to come to the conversation. I wonder if this is where the myth or misinterpretation – the idea of a clear mind – comes from. In one sense, we can clear our mind of our own distractions, but in another sense, we don't want to remove the observations, feelings and thoughts that arise from being in that conversation. If we ignore the mutually created vision of the thinker's world, how are we supporting them to see an expanded view?

So, being present means the coach is deeply engaged in what the client is saying and not saying, noticing the way they narrate the story more than what the story is, and reflecting back what they notice. Presence is built on deep listening and curiosity on behalf of the person speaking. If the coach is to be a conduit for a conversation someone has with themselves, that curiosity should not be focused on the details of the content – that would represent a coach's curiosity about the client. To be curious on behalf of the client is more like sitting alongside them and looking into their world, beliefs, behaviours, fears and dreams, and gently drawing attention to places of connection, disconnection, doubtful beliefs and deeply held values. This curiosity brings things into the light so that the thinker can see them clearly, often for the first time.

Looking into another's world-view may bring up some ethical dilemmas for us as coaches. What if their world-view is coloured by racism, misogyny or other views that oppose our own? Should we challenge them, and if so, when and how? Can we remain truly present and non-judgemental, and indeed should we? I have found no clearly defined answers to these questions, but I fall back on my ability to partner with the other person and hold them in unconditional positive regard. If I can't do that, I cannot be of service to them.

The presence we seek to evoke in others

The feelings our presence evoke in someone will outlive anything we have said or done. How do we want people to feel in our presence? If our aim is to ensure people feel seen, heard and understood, how do we create the environment for that to emerge? Carl Rogers (1957) gave us the necessary and sufficient conditions of a therapeutic relationship:

- There is a psychological contract.
- The client is incongruent.
- The therapist (coach) is congruent.
- The client is held in unconditional positive regard.
- The therapist (coach) has an empathic understanding of the client.
- The client recognizes it.

Others close to Rogers (Carkhuff, 1969) see three of the six original conditions as being 'core' to the therapist's way of being, and we can translate these to the coaching relationship. They are that the coach is congruent or authentic, that they experience unconditional positive regard towards the person they are working with and they are empathic towards them. To be congruent as a coach, we really need to show up in the relationship as our true selves. There is no space for hiding behind masks or pretence. As well as that being disingenuous, it is also futile, as we are working with intelligent people who will quickly recognize the incongruence.

Unconditional positive regard is an interesting one, and a question that often emerges in supervision is: Can I coach someone if I don't like them? One coach I worked alongside once said we don't have to like our clients, but we do have to love them. I spent some time reflecting on what that meant. My current position on the question, that comment and the concept of unconditional positive regard is that in coaching we are partnering with another person to support them to achieve their aims. If, for some reason, I feel I cannot partner with a person wholeheartedly to do that and empathize with their current position and challenges, then I really am not the best person to support them. Where do you stand on the question?

These conditions speak to the trust that another person seeks before they feel able to really explore and challenge themselves with a coach as witness. There are, of course, also the fundamentals of building trust, such as assurance that their truth is safe with you from a perspective of confidentiality and, more than that, trust that you can contain that truth, especially if it comes with strong emotions. Professor Rebecca

Jones (2021) has explored the research related to this need for containment and the deepening of the relationship when emotions such as shame and humiliation arise. As Jones asserts, we all defend against these feelings of shame because it is hard to be confronted with why we have behaviours, thoughts and emotions that can be deeply ingrained in us. These are the ugly parts of ourselves we push into the shadows. Therefore, building the conditions to allow these to surface and be contained will allow for deeper enquiry and revelation.

The messiness of humanity can only safely emerge to the presence of a person who can contain it without being overwhelmed. What happens to you when strong emotion emerges in a coaching conversation? Do you rush past it, fail to give it space? Do you rush to make it better with hugs and tissues, or flinch if the emotions are more aggressive? All these behaviours convey that certain emotions are unwelcome when, to be fully seen, heard and understood, all emotions need to be welcomed and contained in the coaching space.

Flexing your energy

Many coaches talk about containment as a 'safe' space. I refer to it more as a 'brave' space. This bravery is not just about the client's courage but the coach's too. If a coach is deeply engaged and responsive to all that emerges, there will be moments of opportunity to offer stillness, silence or a more disruptive challenge, all of which take confidence and gravitas. There is a dynamic nature to the coach's presence, but this is always in service of the client's needs. Clynes' (1977) concept of sentic states is useful here. He proposes that there are seven basic emotional states or rhythms that are universal across cultures, and when applied to coaching, we can consider how we can flexibly employ these rhythms to support our clients to expand their awareness. The sentic states are:

- Awe – a state appreciating beyond self
- Joy – a celebratory state
- Eros – an excited state
- Love – an inclusive state
- Grief – a state of empathy and surrender
- Hatred – a state of mobilization
- Anger – a boundary-setting state, saying NO

The label for the different states are problematic as they conjure up certain behaviours that are not necessarily appropriate in the coaching space. For example, anger could be misconstrued as an aggressive act. However, the energy associated with the words is more relevant to the presence we can bring to bear on the other person's thinking. Each of us will have a preferred rhythm in coaching. Many may adopt the grief state, that of empathy, providing a calmer space with a slower pace, where the other person can totally surrender. This can be a very useful and accepting space, but to stay there will not move the person forward. For that, we may require anger (see what I mean about the terms?). Think of the energy that might go with anger, it is all about mobilization to action. Peter Hawkins suggests that the music at the beginning of *West Side Story* is the musical equivalent of the energy of anger (Hawkins and Smith, 2013). He offers musical equivalents for all the different energy states to give a sense of the way you can flex your energy to best serve the client's needs.

The mindful shift in our presence between the states of grief and anger would mean that once we fully hear a person with empathy, we encourage them to view the choices available to them. If we stay in empathy, the person may feel better because they have shared their pain with someone, but nothing will have changed. They have friends for that. The disruptive presence of the coach will be less about colluding with the pain and more about acknowledging it and then drawing on the energy of mobilization to support the person to recognize they have choices they can act on.

Similarly, a coach more settled in anger with a preoccupation with getting to results might want to flex their energy to encourage the client to focus on the joy of celebrating the learning and insights they have had. Maybe they could dwell longer in the love energy to view a more inclusive world where they are looking at the world through the difference between them and their client. The key here is to recognize your own preferred approach and then experiment with bringing different energies to bear in service of the client's learning and forward movement. Holding a brave space for your client through being present in a way that is most useful to them requires you to be flexible in the energy you bring to the coaching conversation.

It can be useful to listen carelessly to a recording of your coaching. When I say carelessly, I mean not listening to the client or your interventions, but only to the rhythm of the conversation. Is it all one pace, or are there different energies at different times?

I smile now as I think about how some new coaches become entranced by the content of the 'story' the client presents, meaning they are so preoccupied that they have absolutely no capacity to bring the power of their presence to bear. There is such liberation in recognizing that the story is not where the gold is, and placing one's attention more on being present to what is happening as the person narrates their experience offers far more depth of understanding.

Increasing your presence

There is such comfort in the certainty of a coaching process or model. We can feel so confident when we have them to fall back on. Sadly, I am here to whip that comfort away from you with the truth that nothing is certain and you will only transcend the rules if you are willing to let go of certainty and get comfortable with discomfort. Lots of coaching education encourages coaches to become confident in their being, and this can be interpreted as being in control, which in turn leads coaches to try to plan sessions in advance, think of great and powerful questions or work on their identity as a good coach. But that does not bring coaching confidence.

Confidence in coaching means sitting in that liminal space of ambiguity and uncertainty without the urge to retreat or advance. This is a tough ask for those of us who are invested in adding value, proving our worth and helping people. People turn to coaching to make sense of their life and work. They are intelligent and resourceful. They don't need us to state the blinking obvious with our solutions – they need a thinking partner to help them navigate the emotional and psychological barriers that prevent them from doing what they know they need to do. If we do truly believe that we all have a greater guide in us than anyone else could ever be, then our job is to manage our own insecurities to sit alongside someone while they unravel theirs.

We have a tendency to fall back on tried and tested ways of being when we feel uncertain, and this also happens in coaching. When someone hits a wall of emotion or 'stuckness', it is all too easy to act on our temptation to problem-solve or find the right question. Increasing our presence relies on us being able to notice and resist the temptation to do something to release us from our discomfort. In *The Places that Scare You*, Pema Chödrön (2001) encourages us to adopt the 'warrior in training' mindset. This mindset is the practice of staying open-hearted regardless of the triggers in the prevailing situation that might cause us to close down. For coaching, this means cultivating the art of staying with the discomfort of not knowing without resorting to seeking a solution to make us feel better. This Buddhist concept can help us to enhance our presence by accepting we can never know or plan for what will emerge, but we can call on our courage to role-model leaning into uncertainty, even when the ground beneath us is shaky, to explore unique ways of being and to wait for the client's own wisdom to emerge.

Trusting the process

'Trust the process' is a phrase I heard and resisted early in my coaching career. There was something about 'process' that conjured up manipulation for me and challenged my own ego and identity as a coach. As I have developed the concept of the first and second half of coaching life, I have become more tolerant of the idea of affording the process my trust. If we have learnt the rules – aka the process – we can loosen our grip and trust that we will be holding true, unconsciously, to the general elements of a coaching session. This process will then create the boundaries that will allow us to sit in the unknown with another person without getting lost.

What differences might you notice in the presence of a coach who transcends the rules and the presence of one who is still in the first stage of coaching? The one who transcends the rules will certainly provide a lot more silence and reflective space in the conversation. They will take fewer actions and bring more reflection and sharing of what they notice. If strong emotions emerge, you would see this coach acknowledging them without trying to 'fix' things by offering tissues, placating, offering hugs or positive takes. They would just give a quiet assurance the emotions are seen and possibly check in regarding what meaning the client has attached to them. I hear the term 'holding space' a lot in relation to coaching, and my first thought when I came across that was what the hell does that mean? The best I can offer as an answer is that there is a felt sense that all is well and all emotions are welcome; there is no need to mask anything.

If we are to bring more confidence to our presence, we must get familiar with it and our reactions. The obvious place we go to when working to increase our self-awareness is our thoughts, beliefs and values, missing out a massive piece of the puzzle – that thing that carries our head and thoughts around. There is so much more information about us and our clients that is held in our bodies. If only we would listen to it. I remember asking one client what her gut was telling her, to which she replied, 'I haven't listened to that since 1973.' That's pretty typical, I would say. If our presence is built on deep listening, we need to start by listening to the whole of us: mind, body and spirit.

There is no one route I know of to increase your presence. It requires the tough path of recognizing that control is an illusion. We are all messy humans living in a complicated and messy world, but we can build our capacity to reframe our judgement about what we can and can't control and get curious about where uncertainty takes us. We can start down that path by constantly reflecting on our own motivations for coaching, as discussed in Chapter 2, and then build on that by recognizing the times we are drawn away from discomfort and the times we avoid the scary places, remembering to tap into our intuitions and embodied experience. By embodied experience, I am referring to the bodily sensations that can sometimes go unnoticed. Do you notice a tension or relaxation in your body at certain times? Do you notice yourself feeling warmer, catching your breath or reacting with seemingly automatic movement? All of these can be signals that you are sensing danger and maybe it is time to experiment with pressing onward.

My summary reflections

- My presence is a given; it is there – I don't need to work at it. My only task is to remove the things that get in the way.
- Preparing is about returning to presence, not performance.
- I am responsible for managing my energy in the coaching relationship, and I can flex it to meet the needs of the client.

- Not knowing is something to be welcomed, not avoided.
- My uniqueness may be found in the very thing I have tried to change.

Your reflection prompts

- When and how are you tempted to perform?

- What is your reaction to strong emotions in coaching?

- What energy or rhythm do you think you bring most?

- What energy or rhythm do you think you leave out most?

- What is the coaching identity you hold?

- What would it take for you to let that go?

As you reflect on what you have read, take some time to sit in your own presence and see what emerges from your internal wisdom.

4

The myth of the objective observer

The title of this chapter relates to a question I explored with one of my supervisors, Laurence Barrett – whether the coach can be an objective presence in the process of coaching. In *A Jungian Approach to Coaching*, he asserts: 'Every human relationship is an intersubjective experience' (Barrett, 2023, p. 89). We can't help but be affected by each other in our relationships. People remind us of others and evoke reactions in us, and when working with others, we create an energy between us. Early training programmes encouraged coaches to practise emptying their minds, leading many coaches to ignore their thoughts, feelings and intuition for fear of leading the client. However, it is a myth that this is possible or desirable, and the more we accept that, the better we will become as coaches as we manage ourselves in the relationship.

The benefit of recognizing that you can never be objective is that there is a whole wealth of information available to you when you use your own experience in a conversation. When mentoring coaches for credentials, I regularly notice the opportunities to evoke awareness that they miss due to this misguided belief that to contribute their own observations is leading. Leading is when the coach decides *for* the client – it can be deciding the topic, where to go in the conversation, the best approach or solution, what to explore and what to leave alone. This is totally different from a coach noticing and offering an observation to aid the client's exploration. I always think of this offering as a gift for the client to do with what they wish, a little like making sure there is a gift receipt so unwelcome presents can be returned.

Misconstruing this 'rule' of coaching shows up in a few ways. For example, in one recording I listened to in my role as mentor, I heard the client talk for about 10 minutes about their goal of presenting more powerfully to the board. When I asked the coach what they were thinking and feeling during this time, they offered me a polite response that was suitable for a respectful coach. Pushing further, I asked what was being censored, and this resulted in an exasperated: 'I was thinking, oh for goodness' sake, get on with it!' Now we were at the truth and something useful. How could that sense of losing patience be conveyed respectfully in service of the client? We don't have to speak our internal dialogue out loud, but we should acknowledge that it can signal that there is something here that we should take notice of. Reflecting this to the client is not leading; it is up to them what they do with that information, but it seems disingenuous to ignore what may be the key to someone's increased awareness. As Brené Brown (2021) reminds us, to be clear is kind and to be unclear is unkind.

Is it mine, theirs or ours?

As we explored earlier, we do not enter the coaching conversation as a blank slate – we bring our own stories, values and beliefs, as do our clients. We could spend forever wondering about and trying to disentangle whether what emerges in a relationship is my stuff, or theirs, or are we creating it together? As coaches, we may have an awareness of transference, counter-transference and projection, and we can tie ourselves in knots trying to analyse every conversation and relationship we have. I am indebted to Barrett's no-nonsense approach reminding me we are always in transference when we are in a relationship, or as Jung terms it, 'mutual entanglement' (Barrett, 2023, p. 90).

Our transferences and projections are based on our history and the systems we belong to, and it would be naive of us to think we can leave this behind as we coach. Better to be aware of the response evoked in us by our clients so that we can manage it rather than let it drive our behaviours. We do not need to be psychoanalysts to be great coaches, but we do need to recognize that we all have a dynamic unconscious that is a rich source of information, some of it built on old and worn-out patterns and some of it useful and vibrant. As Catherine Sandler exhorts, we must work to 'observe not suppress' our transference and counter-transference reactions (2011, p. 68).

Sometimes our reactions can feel extreme, even shameful. We can take a dislike to a person based on what may seem superficial reasons and then judge ourselves harshly. Whenever we start to feel uncomfortable with a person, you can be sure that this is exactly when our own personal biases will rear their heads. We can begin to make judgements about whether the person is coachable or not, or the kind of person we want to coach. We might ask ourselves: 'Do I have to like everyone I coach?' With robust supervision and a commitment to reflective practice, working with the people you have a strong reaction to may be exactly what you need. As Pema Chödrön says, 'we work on ourselves in order to help others, but also help others in order to work on ourselves' (2008, p. 56). Rather than spiralling into self-judgement, it is useful to get curious to understand the root of the reactions.

There are so many psychological theories that we can draw on to help us understand the patterns and narratives we bring into our coaching. We could explore our personal childhood story, drawing on Sarah Hill's (2023) work on structural dynamics, for example. Hill asserts that as a child, we all had an internal narrative of imperfect love – even those who had a happy childhood. So a 'star child' may grow into an adult with a narrative of needing to be idolized and noticed, a 'carer child' may be compelled to help, a 'compliant child' may seek to be what others want them to be and so on. Recognizing how this can sneak into our coaching persona is enlightening, as long as we understand the pattern.

As these internal narratives are strongly entrenched, they can surface regularly, especially in what Hill calls 'high stakes' situations. Unexamined, the stories we told ourselves to keep us safe, accepted or valued as a child could get in the way of our coaching. Table 1 shows my interpretation of how each childhood archetype, as identified by Hill, might impact our coaching. Remember, though, that this is only my flawed truth based on my own reflections. I have done no research on this concept. Please read Sarah's book to help you reflect on your ideas about what your own story brings to your coaching. Of course, like everything, there may be rich positive attributes that come with your story; rarely is anything all negative.

Table 1: The potential impact of archetypes in coaching

Archetype	My interpretation of the impact in coaching
The injured child 'Don't hurt me'	Their sensitivity to power abuses may lead them to avoid vulnerability, seek power in the relationship or defend clients they perceive as vulnerable.
The star child 'Notice me'	They may seek to gain praise and adoration from clients, so their performance is key.
The compliant child 'I can't be what everyone wants'	They may want to ensure they are staying firmly within the rules of coaching, getting security from processes and techniques.
The carer child 'I want to help'	They may tend to take responsibility for their clients, worry about them and fail to keep boundaries clear.
The abandoned child 'Everyone leaves me'	They may not value themselves enough to manage their own self-care. They may struggle to cultivate trust in the relationship and have difficulty bringing robust challenge into the conversation for fear of offending and losing a client.
The unfairly accused child 'Please stop blaming me'	They may be sensitive to not making a difference for the client or struggle to allow the client space when issues of fairness come up.

Archetype	My interpretation of the impact in coaching
The 'try harder' child 'I'm scared I'll never be good enough'	They may work hard to ensure there is an outcome in the session. If one technique doesn't work, they may load in more and more in order to achieve success.
The compelled child 'I'm worried I will let you down'	They may take responsibility for the successes and failures of their clients.
The overprotected child 'I'm not okay alone'	They may be risk-averse, which could impact how far they challenge clients beyond their current thinking.
The unrecognized child 'Please see me for who I am'	They may conform to the accepted persona of coach or rebel against it. Either way, they may not be comfortable bringing their true self into the partnership.
The loved and respected child 'I know I'll be alright'	They may feel well-equipped to tackle most things, including unfairness or challenge, and this could be out of synch with the client's reality. They may underplay the struggles of others who are less well-equipped.

Transactional analysis, a psychological model of human interactions that was developed by Eric Berne (2010), offers another perspective that we can use to think about our drivers and how they impact our coaching. Transactional analysis focuses on the unconscious transactions between us when we communicate and offers a lens to view some of the 'games people play', as Berne terms it. He identifies the 'ego' states of parent, adult and child; depending on which ego state is activated, corresponding behaviours, involving collaboration or conflict, can occur. In a coaching conversation, we seek to have an adult-to-adult conversation, although at times there may be a little flexibility to draw on the child's playfulness. There are free online questionnaires that help you get a sense of the ego state that is most familiar for you. Similarly, there are free questionnaires to understand the drivers of our behaviours, learnt in childhood. Be strong, be perfect, try hard, hurry up and please others are all drivers that can unconsciously interfere with our coaching approach if left unchecked. The labels alone conjure up the ways they can influence a conversation.

Similarly, our attachment style can bring both benefits and pitfalls to bear. If we have an anxious attachment in relationships, we can be keen to please and fear rejection. Consider how that could play out in your presence as a coach. You may well be empathic and responsive to needs but fearful of sharing observations for fear of rejection. A coach with a more avoidant attachment style may be great at focusing the work on actions that can be taken while shying away from emergent emotions.

When I consider the legion of influences on my coaching, I can get overwhelmed and self-critical, but that is not the purpose of raising these theories and possibilities here. It is more to raise your awareness of the myriad of factors at play below the surface, the futility of believing you can be an objective observer and the power of drawing on all that is emerging in the conversation as a rich source of data for mutual growth and development. It is also useful to remember all psychological theories are just that: *theories*. They may come with lots of compelling evidence, but they are still only part of the story of who we are. Observing our personalities reminds me of looking through a kaleidoscope; we get a different view with each turn of the dial. Each different theory shows up different aspects of our essence. With all this flying around, I wonder how any coach has time to get entangled in the actual content that comes up in sessions.

Discharging the loyal soldier

Richard Rohr (2012, p. 43) retells the story of the loyal soldier in *Falling Upward*, and this has resonance for our presence as coaches. The story relates to how the Japanese government honoured the returning soldiers at the end of World War Two with ceremonies that thanked them for their service and formally discharged them from their roles so they could reintegrate into society. It reminds me of the need for good endings and purposeful beginnings in all systems. Many of us come to coaching from other professions and roles. Some may have been leaders, consultants, therapists, teachers – we carry so many skills that we were rewarded for in those roles. How can we honour those skills while loosening our grip on ones that are less useful in coaching? Vigilance is key here; we need to be alert for the moments in a coaching conversation when we are seduced into re-enlisting the soldier.

The thing I watch out for and try to avoid is being a teacher, my absolute passion. I have heard so often from coaches that they 'took their coaching hat off', a phrase that gives me the jitters – is this really about helping the client? I wonder if it is more that the coach could see an opening to get to their comfort zone of problem-solving, aka adding value. You don't have to dismiss your experience, but perhaps use it in a different way. Your experience can inform the questions you ask to broaden the other person's thinking, without there being a need for you to change your hat. It could help you to reflect on what is happening when you start to feel yourself straying into old patterns. Is it something the client is inviting from you? That could be worth exploring with them – why they feel your wisdom exceeds theirs.

My summary reflections

- The coaching relationship is a partnership of equals.
- Drawing on my thoughts, observations, feelings and intuitions can bring more awareness to the conversation.
- I bring my history and influences into my coaching awareness.
- Observing the dynamics of the partnership is useful; suppression of them is not.
- My past experience can be useful if used wisely.

Your reflection prompts

- What are the traps you can fall into when coaching based on your past experience?

- How could you use your past training and experience differently in coaching?

- Reflect on a time when you censored what you were thinking. Based on what you know now, what might you have done differently?

5

The implications for presence and mindset

We have looked at just a few areas that might set you on a journey of discovery about yourself and who you are in essence as a coach. This is an ongoing journey, and it can sometimes be exasperating. As some of my colleagues and I often say, everything is an AFLO – another *flipping* learning opportunity (add your own expletive) – and we can get tired of them and overwhelmed. A big spoon of self-compassion is required to help them go down. It is worth repeating here: exchange judgement for curiosity.

It takes time to deepen your self-awareness, and the place to start will become obvious to you if you are paying attention. You will notice a pattern or the same client issue will weirdly keep appearing, often the very issue you are challenged by in your own life. I hope this brief exploration has encouraged you to recognize the necessity for regular and robust supervision to support you to build your awareness.

If you are not yet working with a supervisor, that's okay. Maybe you haven't yet seen the need or felt the draw. Maybe it sounds too much like being called to the headteacher's office in school – she never had anything good to say. I know when I first started, coaching supervision was in its infancy and I was not encouraged to engage in this reflective practice with a more seasoned coach. I know that whenever it was mentioned, I was a little wary, mainly because I had experienced a version of supervision in previous professional roles and I hadn't benefited from it. I had experienced the dread of facing the headteacher, and that old narrative loomed large for a while. I was afraid of harsh judgement. Even worse, I often got to listen to all the latest moans and groans of my supposed supervisor, as they would give me a brief verbal download of my performance and then use the rest of the session as personal therapy time.

How would it feel if you knew that supervision with someone you trusted would be a magical place of self-discovery, a place where you could bring all 'your uglies' and receive nothing but acceptance. If it was a time and space to embrace the mystery of you and coaching in the same way as you explore your life with a trusted friend, would that make it more appealing? I can only share what I get from these times I set aside for my own growth in coaching and the much wider impacts on my life generally.

First and foremost, I get to share my reflections with another person who understands the ground I am working in. In partnership, we explore questions that I have been exploring about myself, the people I work with and our relationships. Together, we think about the decisions I make in coaching – how I came to them and implemented them – and if there is anything we can both learn from that. Sometimes, my supervision session is my time to restore, shake the dust from myself and feel refreshed, ready to go back to work. Sometimes I can discuss particular client situations in confidence to find even better ways to work with them. What I don't get is judgement, shame or humiliation. Ultimately, I always learn so much.

Reflection and supervision are valuable tools to constantly refine and redefine your coaching mindset and presence. You can also reflect with peers or alone through writing, drawing or meditating – whatever helps you to explore what you noticed and what you can learn about yourself from it. This is useful for ongoing reflection but no substitute for working with someone who will be able to guide you further along the road, encouraging you to look at the places you have avoided in your own reflections to seek out the gold in them.

One area for your curiosity is to explore that part of you that you are acutely aware of, that you have been trying to 'cure' for a long time. As the poet David Whyte says in 'Your prayer': 'The part of you you thought was foolish, the wisest voice of all' (Whyte, 2022, p. 35).

This theme runs so much through art, cultures and folklore. Examples include the Japanese philosophy of wabi-sabi, which values simplicity and finds beauty in imperfection, and the kintsugi art form of repairing broken pottery with precious metal powder. Another example is the Navajo belief that the rug weaver's spirit resides in the rug and needs a place to escape, so a deliberate mistake or 'spirit line' is woven into it. The underlying belief is that broken places become a strength, and it is the same for us. What we think is our weakest facet is really our strength if we can but recognize it. Instead, others feedback on our 'weakness' so we feel shame and do even more to hide it, developing unhelpful behaviours. The wisest part of us gets lost in our pretence of perfection. You are aiming to discover the essence of you, and that cannot be uncovered when the shadow part of you is being denied. It's a life's work uncovering all our shadows and sometimes we need help, but continual reflection can start the process and allow you to bring more of yourself to your coaching relationships.

Writers and philosophers have presented the idea of our innate wisdom in a variety of ways. One interpretation I heard from Michael Neill in one of his coaching masterclasses is the concept of the diamond and nail polish. His story reminds me of the experience I had when I gave birth to my oldest daughter, Claire. I was in a maternity ward with three other women. We all had very different lives. I remember getting very philosophical – I think it was a combination of drugs and hormones – imagining these four perfect babies going off to vastly different lives and what that would mean for them.

Michael Neill expresses this perfection as a diamond we are all born with, residing at the heart of us, beautiful, shining and perfect – and then life happens. We grow up in families where, regardless of intent, we experience imperfect love and begin to learn who we are from what others say we are. These labels overlay the diamond. School adds another layer to the understanding of self. Peers, partners, work colleagues all add to the mix of stuff dulling the shine. Some of those labels can feel like dirt and we start to feel ashamed, so we metaphorically paint over the dirt with nail polish, trying to overcome the negative beliefs and attributes others have assigned to us. We think we are broken or at least not perfect, so we need to mask that in some way. We cover up to make sure no one sees our shame, and we work hard to become what we think makes us perfect when, in truth, all we need to do is clean off the diamond and remember that we are perfect just as we are. In fact, as David Whyte intimates in his poem 'Your Prayer', the faults you are trying to mask are likely to be your very gift to the world. So instead of trying to cover over the cracks, maybe our job as coaches is to reflect on them and see how they can be an asset in our work.

You will eventually find an approach to reflection that suits you, but as Professor Steve Peters (2020) advises in *The Chimp Paradox*, settle on an achievable time commitment – about 10 minutes a day – to make it a habit. One approach I favour is free writing all that I am thinking and feeling in relation to anything that comes up in my coaching or life. I then summarize that into a question I pose for myself and sit quietly with that question or sometimes hold the question in my mind while I take an exercise class. I truly believe there is a deeper part of us that already knows the answer, and it can only emerge when we silence the nagging of the gremlin in our mind. Sometimes the question doesn't leave me, so that is one I take to my supervision sessions.

Reflection and self-awareness are worthwhile in and of themselves, but the focus here is on the impact this work has on our coaching. If we are to bring all of ourselves to our craft, we really need to know what we are bringing and manage it. If we don't understand and transform our hurts and triggers in some way, we will project them into our coaching.

As we come to the end of this chapter, let's add in another opportunity for reflection. Please take a moment to tune in to your own intuition and wisdom.

My summary reflections

- There is a difference between striving to improve my skills and striving for perfection.
- The difference lies in learning for the love of it and hoping to prove my worth.
- I will project whatever I don't transform onto my coaching relationships.
- Spending time on reflection is not another stick to thrash myself with; it's enough to ponder in whatever way works and whenever its useful.

Your reflection prompts

- Is there something that you believe stops you being perfect?

- If you accept you will never be perfect, how does that feel?

- What would happen if you viewed your biggest perceived flaw as your gift to coaching?

As we come to the end of Part 1, why don't you take a few moments to reflect on all that you have read and consider what your own wisdom is saying to you now. Remember, you don't have to accept it all – whatever thoughts have arisen will have taught you something or provoked new insights. Make a note of anything you feel is significant here.

Your freshest thinking

Part 2

Curious acceptance of difference

6

Building a brave space for exploration

The longer I coach, the more I value the importance of building a partnership with the client. This coaching alliance has been shown to be key to the success of coaching (De Haan et al., 2011), and yet its importance can sometimes be missed by coaches just starting out. If the person seeking coaching is going to have the conversation they need to have with themselves, they will need to be confident in the person witnessing and supporting them. In my role as Programme Director for accredited programmes, I was always keen to share the importance of this foundational stage of the coaching relationship. To help the coaches on those programmes remember the key elements of the conversation to build an effective relationship for the work, I created the mnemonic PROMISES. I offer an abridged version in Table 2.

As a coach wanting and needing to build a business, it is so tempting to work with whomever asks. I hope you are a little more restrained than I was in the first months and years after my training, when I thought coaching was a panacea for anything. No issue was too small or too big for me to stomp in with my size seven boots and a tool bag, full of delusions that I could save the world one coaching conversation at

Table 2: PROMISES: Building an effective relationship

P	**Purpose:** What brought the person to coaching, and what did they hope to achieve through it?
R	**Relationship:** What brought them to you specifically? What are they seeking from a coach? How do they like to work? How do you like to work?
O	**Outcome:** How do they envision a successful outcome of coaching, and what are their hopes for the relationship?
M	**Margins:** 'Boundaries' would be a better way to describe this, but 'B' does not fit into the mnemonic. What is up for discussion, and what is not? How will you maintain boundaries that work for both?
I	**In case:** We can never know what will emerge in coaching, so we can never cover all eventualities. How will you deal with emerging issues? Have a 'what will we do if…' conversation.
S	**Strategy:** This is the 'how' of the relationship – the general logistics of how you will work together with the client. How often will you meet? How much will you charge?
E	**Expectations:** This is about unearthing any psychological contracts we can enter into unwittingly – for example, when someone really expects you to have the answers.
S	**Safety:** This is about building a safe working alliance that has clarity about confidentiality and its limits, and a revisiting of boundaries that creates safe containment for both.

a time. My only pre-coaching conversation with potential clients was aimed at converting them to booked ones. This approach created lots of learning, which I hope was not at the expense of those brave clients, though I am sure some would have been better served by another coach or intervention.

My approach has now changed to one where I engage in this initial conversation with the sole intent of supporting the other person to get the best support for them, and that may not be through me. It's been a long time since I experienced the angst of working hard to meet needs that I am not really equipped to deal with or felt anything but joy at the thought of working with any of the people I coach. That means I can bring my best self to the initial conversations, and this gives the person seeking support the time and space for reflection on the best way to get it. If we both decide we can build a useful working alliance, my mantra is always: 'What's the work we need to do, and how shall we do it?'

When I think of the working alliance or partnership being created in coaching, I think of all the other partnerships in my life and how I have bumbled into some pretty major partnerships without this level of discussion. For example, 46 years of marriage started a bit like my early coaching – there was no consideration of what assumptions we both might be holding; it was just: did I want to get married? I am sure others operate without the impulsivity of my ADHD brain – nevertheless, if we are going to enter into the 'covenant' or 'sacred promise' that Blakey and Day (2012) term the 'coaching contract', then we need to give it some careful consideration. Thankfully, luck, patience and a big dollop of humour allowed our marriage to survive and thrive, but hoping for good luck is not the best plan for beginning a coaching relationship.

An area of conversation that is imperative is planning for the unknown. It is so much easier to have a preparatory conversation before something happens than to try to manage retrospectively – this relates to the 'in case' element of PROMISES. This can be viewed as gaining permission to bring yourself and what you notice into the conversation and to devise a way to navigate it in partnership. It may be permission to share something about the other's way of being or their behaviours or it may be a breach of boundaries or expectations – all uncomfortable issues that coaches struggle to navigate when they arise unexpectedly in a coaching relationship. Similarly, the client needs an easy way to raise subjects about the coach's way of being or behaviour that is not working for them. Planning a way to have those necessary conversations makes it so much easier; like a marriage or business partnership entered into with eyes wide open, it prevents a lot of the awkwardness.

As coaches, we can role-model planning for difficult conversations. Think about all the coaching conversations that are aimed at supporting clients to manage miscommunications or relationship issues in their work and life. How useful would it be to learn from inside a partnership that is built to withstand radical honesty and deal with emerging issues with curiosity, courage and compassion for the other and clarity on how to raise issues so that they land well with the other person?

Transcending the relationship rules goes beyond the logistics of what coaching is and isn't. Of course, there is an element of that, but a deep connection needs more than a list of rules. Asking 'Why coaching?' and 'Why me?' can really get to the heart of the matter. Coaching doesn't start after this first conversation; it starts so much earlier. Whenever I have sought a coach, supervisor or mentor, there have been days or weeks of internal meandering beforehand, much more than I spent thinking about getting married. What drew me to that person at that time? What was I secretly hoping I would get from them? I love to believe that magic is afoot, bringing me to the right person at the right time, but my psychological training dispels that romance and assures me there is something far less supernatural going on. If we want to transcend the rules but keep a process in mind, we can build a transformative partnership, but we need to understand the thought process that brought the person to us.

As part of a relationship, the client will want to connect with the real and messy part of you, just as you want to connect to this aspect of them. This is the reason why coaches need to work on their self-awareness. I hate the expression and the whole transactional concept behind the 'elevator pitch'. I do though recognize the need to be able to convey succinctly who you are as a coach. I have heard so many coaches say how empathic they are or how well they listen, or maybe they refer to how well they empower people or even offer approaches they take in coaching. But none of that tells me who they are. I don't have the formula for a powerful 'pitch', but I do urge you to consider your earlier reflections and what that means for who you are, and are not, as a coach so that you can convey it clearly. Our foibles are just as important as our values to another person considering working with us. I know that in my way of connecting, I really don't fit the 'approved' way of being. I share my own experiences and tell stories from my own life – it's how my brain connects. People I work with now tell me they value that; but not everyone does, so it is best to know upfront how someone likes to work with a coach.

This initial conversation is as much about the coach feeling happy to proceed as it is for the client to feel happy to continue. If you are still building your business, it may seem like a no-brainer to take on every client that comes along. That is your choice; in my experience, ignoring any misgivings you have about your compatibility with a client leads to hard work and misery. Once I was clear how I like to work and, just as importantly, how I don't like to work, it was so much easier to work only with people that I knew I could be of service to. Many years ago, someone came to me through another coach, who had a totally different approach to me. I didn't do any of this early 'contracting' and just jumped into the first session. We weren't too far in when the person stopped and said they didn't like the way we were working. It was far too psychological. She just needed me to tell her what to do. We agreed to abandon the session, and I learnt my lesson.

Above all, the precious first conversation can be a dynamic example of what coaching will be like with you, more than your words or 'rules' of coaching could ever be. If you can show up without an agenda of gaining a new client and be seen to encourage the client to show themselves, you are laying the foundations for the conversation the person needs to have with themselves. Then you can build a working alliance that will make a difference.

My summary reflections

- The initial conversation is all about getting to know each other and checking for compatibility.
- It is far easier to explore how to manage difficult situations before they arise than to find out after they come about.
- It pays to be discerning about who you work with, for their benefit and your own.
- Checking why the person thought you would be a good fit gives lots of useful information for the partnership.

Your reflection prompts

- Who would be your ideal client, and why?

- Who would be the worst coaching client you can imagine, and why?

- What would you have to believe to allow you to take each coaching enquiry as an exploration rather than an opportunity to sell?

7

Birdwatching for coaches

We don't know who discovered water, but we're pretty sure it wasn't a fish.

Author unknown

It is a constant source of wonder to me how differently we all see the world and still believe it provides a solid, objective, unchangeable experience. Our reality is coloured by our life stories and experiences, so we see the same objective world through different prisms and, more importantly, we react as if our version is true. No wonder we, as coaches, need to be comfortable with 'not knowing'. We can only know what another person is truly seeing or experiencing if we ask them. The more fascinating thing about this is that we are not even that sure about our own version of the world until someone else draws it to our attention. A commonly used comparison is of the fish being totally unaware of the water it swims in; it would need to be out of the water to notice it.

To carelessly mix metaphors, I think of the coaching relationship as birdwatching, but observing with fascination how people interact with their world and their reality. I don't see this as a lone pursuit; rather, it's a shared experience, with the coach and the client looking from the hide, both noticing and trying to understand what makes this unique being tick. Two sets of eyes with different views getting curious. This joint endeavour is important. It is not one set of eyes looking down or up at the life in front of them. Questions are asked from a place of curiosity to really understand rather than judge. That's why it's important to build a relationship that can contain that curiosity.

This contrasts with the rules of coaching, which might lead us to challenge limiting beliefs or seek other core values, and behaviour change theories, which might lead us to seek the best place to offer a challenge – all useful first-half-of-coaching-life approaches, but with a one-up perspective with one set of eyes looking at the situation and deciding what could be changed or challenged. Going beyond this, transcending would be more about noticing and exploring how that belief or behaviour grew and together wondering which parts of that are still useful and which are not, and what to do about the latter. The three major professional bodies that have competency frameworks all see raising awareness and encouraging insight and learning as core skills of the coach. I will go so far as to say that if someone leaves a coaching session with no more awareness than they had when they came in, they have not really experienced coaching. This gives a purpose to curiosity; it is curiosity on behalf of the client, not about them. The less experienced coach might be curious about the client and ask questions for their own greater understanding of the context, the problem or dilemma – but surely these sorts of questions would lead someone to believe the coach needs such information in order to solve the issue. Instead, transcending that curiosity beyond our own understanding and focusing it on awakening insights for the client will help them to view the world through new eyes and see new possibilities, and they can decide what to do with what they see.

I had some specialized coaching following my ADHD diagnosis, where I gained lots of insight into my world beyond the water I swim in daily. One small and profound insight still smacks me in the middle of my forehead. After decades of battling procrastination, my coach and I noticed that like a lot of people with a neurodivergent profile, I view time differently than a lot of other people. There is very little nuance in my relationship with time. There is now and not now, and like object permanence in infants, not now stuff doesn't really exist until the 'oh crap' energy kicks in. Presenting my procrastination issue to a coach who was less interested in viewing my world alongside me may have resulted in a focus on curing my procrastination 'problem'. It wouldn't have mattered how great the coach was at helping me set realistic planning goals and action plans, I wouldn't follow them, whether or not I rated them highly. I wonder how many times coaches have decided I was not coachable because I didn't complete the actions I agreed to. I needed to see my relationship with time before I could find my way to work with it. But with the perspective of the coach I worked with, I was able to see that I am absorbed in a world where time has a specific meaning – something I wouldn't have been able to do alone.

Neurodivergence is just one of the myriad ways we are all unique. We cannot be an expert in all areas of difference to match our approach to the client's needs. The axiom that we must walk a mile in another's shoes to empathize is not so helpful here. I recall working in community action many years ago and there were projects where people could have experiences that mimicked living with disabilities, such as wearing eyewear that created the effect of certain visual impairments or taking wheelchairs on obstacle routes. This offered one perspective of the superficial difficulties some people face, but it could never convey the lived experience of living in a world created for people with totally different abilities to you, with all the subsequent discrimination. We can never truly know and feel in the same way as another. All we can do is be with the other person, listen to them and observe to get a sense of their truth. None of us is working with absolute reality.

From the shared vantage point of the hide, we can be a critical friend to the person we are coaching. Our aim is not to deny their reality but, with genuine curiosity, help them to see it fully and allow them to question themselves. Our curiosity may lead us to transcend the rules to some degree when we think a little bit of information might help the person view something differently. My coach offered me a piece of information I didn't possess about how other people with ADHD view time, which broadened my horizon and brought other possibilities into view. I know there will be other coaches who would see this as closer to mentoring, and there is a fine line that can be crossed if we stray too far, but that minor intervention was the gift that I may or may not have ever got to through questions alone. It was my choice what to do with that information.

You will decide where you stand on that rule. It seems an ethical question for me. We assume the other person is all-resourceful and can find the answers given the time and space. But what if they really don't have an answer, or even any idea where to start? How ethical is it to leave someone floundering? If this is a partnership, an alliance, to support the other person to think more expansively, wouldn't it be only natural to engage with the subject and make contributions as offers? Such offers come from the coach's truth – not *the* truth – offered only as a prompt to bring more awareness that can be used or ignored.

It's no different to offering observations while looking at the person's life, beliefs and behaviours – for example: 'I notice your energy shift every time you mention that' or 'How does that belief help or hinder you?' A question I find popping into my mind regularly as I survey another's world with them is stolen from the work of Sarah Hill (2023): 'Where did you learn to behave like that?' My job is merely to be curious to help the person think, not to decide what should or shouldn't be different.

My summary reflections

- We all view the world differently, and it is intriguing to look into the world of another with curiosity.
- None of us have 'the truth', just our own version of truth.
- Sharing my thoughts, feelings, intuitions or observations is a gift that can be returned unused.

Your reflection prompts

- When was the last time you questioned any of your own deeply held beliefs?

- What was that experience like for you?

8

Fearing the unknown

I think the soul longs, perhaps more than anything else to express itself and be heard or seen. It doesn't need to be fixed, or told what to do next, or given a solution. It simply longs to be witnessed.

Aboodi Shabi (2023)

My dear friend and colleague Aboodi shared this thought with me in one of our many discussions about the art of coaching. Culture, gender, sexuality, social class and religious beliefs all play a part in our personal story, so as coaches we cannot hope to understand all the nuances of our client's life. How can you sit alongside someone and observe their world, beliefs and behaviours with curiosity, respect and wonder? I recall something the late Professor Paul Brown said at a masterclass on coaching that I attended, which I applied the very next day in a coaching session. He was talking about connection in coaching and suggested that a great starting point was merely to ask a client to tell you about themselves. As I met my new client for our first session the next day, quite by coincidence he asked if I would like to hear about his life. Before hearing Professor Brown's perspective, I might have politely worked to focus the client on more current subjects, but instead I heard so much about the values, motivations and drivers of this person through the vivid description he gave of his early life, and it was so useful in our work together.

As it happened, this life I listened into had some similarities to my own, so there were points of connection as well as other elements that were different. It can sometimes be a little harder to stay fully present when there are similarities in background or a presenting issue with the person you are working with. Have you ever noticed you can quickly fall into a sense of knowing the end of the story when you hear the familiar being replayed? That's the danger point. We can switch into a mode that tells us we know what this is about and where it's going. It's normal. Our brains are wired for similarities and differences. But it can also offer us a little reminder to get more curious when we get that sense.

What happens to you when the other person has a life that you have no experience of? If you respond to that question from your 'good coach' stance, you might be thinking you get curious or something equally noble. When I think about all the differences I encounter in the people I coach, there are so many reactions that I have. I am a white woman born in the 1950s in a northern mining village, with a very strong Yorkshire accent. I left school at 14 with no qualifications, making up for that lack of education many years later. This history helped me create lots of stories and assumptions about people from different backgrounds and life experiences. That's ironic really, because one of my pet hates is people making assumptions about me based on my characteristics and stereotypes. We can talk the talk of equality and treating everyone the same, but as coaches we need to consider where we are working from assumptions and stereotypes to the detriment of our clients and the coaching profession.

Roche and Passmore (2021) share thoughts from their research respondents about the impact of colour blindness, meaning that those who are BIPOC (Black, Indigenous and people of colour) are left feeling that a major part of their identity and life story is ignored or dismissed. Similarly, people within the LGBTQIA2S+ community can be left feeling unseen or unheard, if we continue to believe that one size fits all. And we swim in the water of white supremacy and patriarchy, so it's interesting that the coaching profession, which is predominantly made up of women, has a disproportionate number of white male gurus. As post-pandemic coaching is more global than ever, since we have become more familiar with remote meetings and conversations, how can we transcend our own cultural norms to work more inclusively?

I know many of the coaches I have trained or supervised find this an uncomfortable topic. I find it uncomfortable to write about too. I believe there may be similarities in the reasons for the discomfort, and one seems to be a fear of offending, of getting it wrong. I know I feel there is such a lot I don't know or understand, but as willing as I am to learn, I don't know what I don't know. In their 15-point recommendations, Roche and Passmore (2021) suggest that, as coaches, we can seek to broaden and deepen our understanding of diversity in race. We can extend this to include all protected groups, and through increasing our sensitivity and cultural competence we can become allies willing to challenge the people we work with to do the same.

Committing to understanding and building our cultural sensitivity requires us to notice our own assumptions and beliefs and be radically honest about them. Exploring our fear of offending through ignorance enables us to find a way to connect with respect and mutual curiosity. This reinforces the need to build a strong partnership to allow for open discussion and for the coach to be comfortable with not being the expert. You can be sure that when you are feeling at your most vulnerable as a coach, all your beliefs and assumptions will come out to play if you have not worked through them.

My summary reflections

- We can only empathize with another when we hear their lived experience.
- We all come to relationships with our biases and assumptions.
- It is my job to become culturally sensitive. No one is required to teach me.

Your reflection prompts

- How much do you really know about the life of your current coaching clients?

- What assumptions might you be holding about them?

- How can you broaden and deepen your understanding of diversity, inclusion and social justice?

As Part 2 draws to a close, where is your wisdom taking you now?

Your freshest thinking

Part 3

The pathway to co-creation

9

Transcending the rules in practice

This is your call to draw on your courage to apply your learning and get comfortable with discomfort. It's important to be clear here that the coaching you have been doing to date is not wrong and doesn't need fixing; it is most likely your first-half-of-coaching approach, and we all go through this stage. Remember, we must learn the foundational skills and rules so that we can transcend them artfully. As you put into practice what you have learnt in your foundational coaching education, you will start to notice if you are ready to step into the second half of coaching. It may be that all you needed to reflect on is your own thoughts, motivations and internal narrative to free you up to become a more artful coach. If so, great. What follows are some thoughts about some of the stretches to explore. They are not rules or even advice, just some of my own thoughts, which are as fallible as anyone else's.

It may seem that it's taken a while to get to the practical application of all your learning and reflection, but that is exactly the point. Once you have dug deep into who you are and your unique flavour as a coach, the 'how' of applying your special brand of magic becomes simpler. You will be beginning to step into the second half of your coaching life, looking at your skills in a new light and with more grounded confidence to 'just be' rather than relying on the whiz and bang of tools and techniques. In fact, as I begin to write this, I wonder what else would be useful, because once you have dug deep to work on your own ability to sit alongside someone without the need to perform, what else is there? Even so, a pragmatic look at transcending the rules will be useful to consider some of the first-half-of-coaching-life challenges that coaches come across and reflect on them from a fresh perspective. Each of the chapters in this part considers a core coaching skill and addresses some common dilemmas coaches face. The exploration offers thoughts on addressing those dilemmas, but these are not replacement rules, merely reflection points to help you consider your own approach.

Rule-breaking sounds very grand, a bit anarchic, and I do have an ambiguous relationship with rules. Part of me loves a rule to be clear about what is required, but there is also a part of me that kicks against them. I hear from a lot of coaches who are working to complete an International Coaching Federation credential that at the same time as seeking the badge, they are frustrated by the stranglehold the competency framework has on their coaching. Sadly, what emerges from this love-hate relationship in coach development is that some coaches regard a performance evaluation like a driving test that, once passed, means they can then go their own way. Without these coaches having a deep well of experience and knowledge to draw on, this is a worrying development in a profession where we are working with the complexity of the lives of others.

There are lots of training schools that ardently enforce one or more competency frameworks. There are also many academics who actively speak against these, seeing them as a reductionist approach to coaching (Garvey, 2011; Garvey and Stokes, 2022). Tatiana Bachkirova (2015) argues that competency frameworks devalue the art of coaching, reducing them to a set of behaviours. However, there is a need for some form of assurance that coaches are working effectively and ethically, so until a better system of assurance is available, professional coaches will need to find their own solid ground to stand on and the competencies from the professional bodies may offer a starting place. I am not suggesting anarchy here, and we need to understand the rules deeply so that we can transcend them effectively.

De Haan et al. (2011) interviewed 71 executive coaching clients at the beginning of their coaching engagement and reinterviewed 31 of them later. The purpose was to understand what made a difference from a client's perspective. The coaches' personalities and ways of being were key, and what was interesting was that once the working alliance was built, the clients were less interested in what the coaches did as long as they listened, understood and encouraged, offering the right approach at the right time. This suggests that strict adherence to a competency framework does not necessarily guarantee good or great coaching; nor is there much evidence to suggest that those with a badge of mastery in coaching are any better than other coaches. As David Drake (2011) points out, the competencies, like cooking ingredients, require artistry to produce the magic. To get to this level of artistry, he suggests coaches need to grow their technical ability and knowledge alongside their personal maturation.

So where does this leave us in our development, if we seek to be artisans of our craft? Do we ignore the core competencies or apply them in our own sweet way, or do we learn the rules of the game and then break them with artistry? As reductive as the competencies are, they do offer a starting point and a framework for the process of coaching.

My summary reflections

- The real magic in coaching comes from working in the moment in partnership with the client to meet their needs.
- Following a set of rules or competencies does not make one a good coach.
- We need a foundational framework to keep us working professionally and ethically.

Your reflection prompts

- What coaching rules have you been tempted to break, and why?

- How can you discern what is best for your client?

10

Getting to the heart of the matter

Most coaches at the beginning of their learning are taught Graham Alexander and Sir John Whitmore's GROW (goal, realities, options, way forward) model (see Whitmore, 2009) – maybe some of the more seasoned coaches groan at this still being a cornerstone of coach education. We all learn of the importance of defining the goal before embarking on any exploration, and Whitmore encourages us to make those goals courageous. It's interesting that the model found greatest prominence in his groundbreaking book *Coaching for Performance* (Whitmore, 2009). It could be argued that GROW is perfect in performance coaching. Where do you want to go? Where are you now? What are the options? What will you do, and when, to get there? All great places to focus on the 'do it bigger, better, faster' approach. That's probably why it has gotten so much traction in corporate environments. But what if bigger, better, faster is not the goal?

In the current climate in both corporate life and coaching, there are major shifts. Anecdotally, coaches are reporting that much of their work in leadership and executive coaching is focused on well-being and resilience. In coaching, the rise of AI means the more transactional coaching of performance can be handled more economically through AI coaching programs or through a range of technically enhanced platforms that provide lower-cost coaching on an industrial scale. There is still much debate in the coaching community about what this means for coaches. There will always be a place for the more humanistic approach, for coaching that is much more personal and fundamental to people surviving and thriving in times of pressure and uncertainty. That means coaches will need to be prepared to work much more deeply with their clients on the meaningful goals they bring around life, purpose and meaning. Very often, people seeking coaching are not clear themselves about what they want to achieve, and a formulaic process is unlikely to get to the heart of the matter.

As a coach mentor over many years, the consistent area for growth I have seen with coaches at every level of experience is establishing the focus for a session. The goal that a person first presents is rarely the actual subject they want to explore. Think of it like a trip to a doctor with a mildly embarrassing question. We usually wait for that door handle moment before asking it. We might talk about something loosely related first and only as we are about finished dare to say, 'While I am here, could I ask you…?' The poet David Whyte expressed this beautifully in a webinar recently when he said that the conversation you begin with is never the conversation that is needed (the webinar was part of training I completed with Coaches Rising). What we need to do is invite our clients to the edge of that deeper conversation.

The confession

Carl Jung expressed this as needing to get to 'the confession'. This is not to be confused with confession of any religious ritual or legal wrongdoing; rather, it is the voicing of that deep-felt truth that is troubling to the soul. Getting to the essence of the conversation a person needs to have yields a sense of deep release for both coach and client, a sense of 'ah, there it is'. The ability to bring someone to that edge, or confession, is built on trust, safety and the confidence and skill of the coach to stay in potential discomfort with the person they are working with until they get that felt sense.

The confidence to get to the confession could be described as the coach having the courage to call it when they sense there is something not quite right about the proffered topic or goal for the session, or to hold the client firmly with compassion until they can touch that previously hidden place. For example, one client I worked with talked about wanting to spend our time together developing an action plan for a project. That was fine, but he knew I was not a coach who particularly worked in this field and, more importantly, he was a very successful project manager. So what did he think we could do together that he couldn't do alone? It sounded a little like there could be 'haemorrhoids' in the room that were being ignored.

Another person talked about wanting to get ideas from me on leadership strategies. In earlier days in my career, I may have given a speech about the difference between coaching and mentoring, breaking our rapport and trust. Instead,

I asked him to tell me about his experience of leadership. It was clear from his response that he was an experienced leader who had developed many strategies. When I shared my curiosity with him about what he thought I knew that he didn't, we got to the goal beneath the goal – he wasn't sure whether he wanted to stay as a leader or return to his first love as a clinician. Now we had something to work on.

I would like to share some thoughts with you about how you might experiment with getting to the goal beneath the goal, in the spirit of reflection. This is not about setting out a process, but more an intention to prompt your thinking about how you might begin your coaching conversations and navigate some of the typical issues coaches face at this point in a session. The development areas coaches raise for this crucial stage of the coaching conversation are:

- Avoiding a download from the client at the beginning that takes up all of the time
- Managing the balance between getting to the heart of the matter and dipping too far into the content too early
- Managing complex, ambitious or multiple topics
- Getting clarity on a successful outcome and being clear that the goal beneath the goal has been reached

There may be more that you are reflecting on, but let's see if an exploration of these topics helps you with your unique challenge. It may be useful for us to reflect on what we are trying to do at the beginning of the conversation. If you find your 'why', the 'how' may come more easily.

The goal of goal setting

I remember that when I first started coaching, I had a particular mindset in relation to beginning a coaching session; it was essentially: 'let me get through this bit so I can get to the real work'. It took an embarrassingly long time before it dawned on me that this stage of the coaching session *was* the real work. The longer I have been coaching, the more crucial I have found the foundational stage of the coaching relationship and conversation to be. We considered the relationship earlier, so this part will concentrate on the session. I want to emphasize that for all the people I have mentored, from new coaches to those seeking a mastery credential, the biggest improvement I have seen in their coaching is when they get really clear about the beginning of each coaching session and treat it with the reverence it deserves. Blakey and Day (2012) explore contracting in *Challenging Coaching*. They reflect on the agreement between the coach and their client as a covenant or a sacred promise. But what are we promising?

Your personal reflections on your presence and mindset will now begin to impact how you approach this stage of coaching. Knowing that we may be responsible *to* our client but not responsible *for* them and their success should start to liberate you from the need to perform. The mission is to support your client to learn something about themselves or the situation they are exploring, not to learn from you. You will now have more clarity on the boundaries you want to keep strong, and maybe the promise is intrinsic in this combined mindset. Our task, then, is to focus the work to support the client.

I find it useful to consider what the work is that we are trying to achieve in setting a focus for the session. Maybe the word goal is not as helpful as it could be here. When I think about this word, it is loaded with all sorts of thoughts, images and feelings for me. It conjures up a sense of urgency and expectation, and I start to feel uncomfortable that I am going to have to work towards an action plan, which is not my preference. Ultimately, for each coaching session, the aim of the beginning of the conversation is to identify what the work is that needs to be done and understand how it will be done. The focus is to support the client to identify what would be most useful for them to explore so that they can have some kind of shift in their thinking or behaviour that feels right for them. It is the time to gain an understanding about what the person feels is getting in the way of them achieving the shift alone. This takes exploration, sometimes involving going down dead ends and other times following really fruitful paths.

A metaphor that may help is that of a golden thread that we are supporting the client to create at the beginning of their journey. We might even weave a lovely pattern together with the thread that represents the desired outcome. Then the client hands that precious gold thread to us as they embark on their exploration. In some ways similar to the story of how Ariadne saved Theseus from the Minotaur in the Labyrinth by giving him a thread to follow back to the opening of the cave, the coach holds the thread for the thinker while they wander through the different avenues of thought, but always keeping them close to the thread. Of course, that metaphor breaks down a little if the subject matter changes, but maybe that just means a different thread is started.

Getting a word in edgeways

How many times have you met with a coaching client and said 'Hi, how are you?' only to be on the receiving end of a full minute-by-minute account of everything that has happened since you last met? It is a typical conundrum, and the problem is that you can find yourself drawn into a coaching session with no idea of where you are going or why. I wonder if this is the start of the continued confusion about the coaching session. It can seem like any other conversation unless we purposefully manage the process. Of course, none of us want to be so process driven that we don't have time for the social niceties, but there can be a politeness in the coach that takes over and they can feel trapped and unable to get a word in edgeways to focus the conversation.

We can prepare our clients to enter this different kind of conversation when we are establishing the agreement for our coaching relationship. There is a balance to be struck here between keeping focus and letting the person say what they need and want to say to begin the session. Normal rules of conversation are suspended in some ways. One of the responsibilities of the coach is to manage the process, which is easier to do from a confident and grounded place of being clear that this is a purposeful conversation. Small, often subliminal changes to our language – perhaps merely changing a word or two – can set the tone. Consider the difference between asking 'What would you like to talk about today?' and 'Where shall we focus our attention today?'

Another subtle change that can challenge coaches is the ability to interrupt. This is not only a taboo in polite conversation but a rule drilled into coaches in training: don't interrupt.

This is a great example of when transcending the rules can really help. Of course, we don't want to get into the habit of closing clients down by interrupting for no reason, but there are times when it is more helpful to them if we do gently nudge them to what is most useful for them. The skill is knowing the difference. My own rule of thumb is that I don't want to close them down from thinking, but that storytelling or reporting is less useful for them. For example, giving a full report of everything that has happened since the last session is far less useful than what they learnt from it about themselves or the situation, so I will intervene to ask about just that. You may want to experiment with your own ways of intervening, when appropriate, to ensure the person gets the most out of your time together. Simply prompting in the middle of a download with 'What does that suggest would be useful for today?' or even better 'And for today?' will not feel like an interruption given the right relationship and contracting.

Surging too early

Often a coach following a process or model will hear something approximating a goal at the beginning of a session, think they have ticked the box of identifying a goal or outcome and run with it. Models can be useful memory aides, but all too often they are used formulaically, and the result is that the person never gets to that felt sense of confession. A change of mindset to acknowledge this crucial element of the session as the work rather than a precursor helps to slow down the process to understand the essence or heart of the matter. Slowing down means getting curious about the subject and desired outcome, what makes it important now, what will achieving the outcome mean for the person and what would be even more meaningful than that? There can be a temptation to start working on the issue once you start to unpick the subject, so there is a case for managing yourself and the client at this point to stay focused on the 'what' before getting sucked in. This is a delicate balance that takes experimentation and practice, but keeping the intention front of mind helps.

Seeing the wood through the trees

It can be difficult to know what we want from a coaching session and what a good outcome would be like. Our lives do not fall into neat little boxes where we address one challenge at a time. Often issues are related, and one desired change can have many contributing factors. The rules of coaching encourage us to get specific and focused, and this can lead to coaches asking questions such as: 'Of those three things, which would you like to focus on today?' There's nothing wrong with that, but it does suggest that life's complexity can be managed by splitting things up. Transcending that rule might lead us to accept life's complexity.

I invite the client to rise a level above their current thinking, asking things like 'How do you see those three things connecting?' or simply repeating the specific words used and either asking for or offering a connecting word. If we really want to add value, then we at least need to encourage our clients to dig deep into the real subject and stay with it until we get that felt sense that this is meaningful and important and that there is commitment to do something about it.

What we are aiming for

The same principle applies to the desired outcome. Quickly grasping the first thought of what would make the session successful will more often than not result in a transactional session without a meaningful focus that can be checked on at the end. Remember, the desired outcome is the golden thread that will keep you both on track, and it is for the session only. This is a simple fact that often gets missed. What are we aiming for by *the end of the session*? A financial director may say she wants to transition to chief executive in her next career move, but that is not going to happen by the end of the session. It may be a reality by the end of the relationship or she may at least be on her way, but not by the end of session. What will she know, have or feel by the end of your time together that will be useful as a next step? How can she be confident she has achieved that?

Hitting the sweet spot

Remember that this is a crucial element of the coaching and all of your coaching skills will be employed to get a great beginning. Investing time and focus here will save so much time for the essence of the conversation rather than time being wasted on side issues. Read and notice your 'felt' sense from the following example.

> A doctoral student says that what she wants from her coaching session is to feel comfortable the next time she is with her supervisor. The coach asks what comfortable would feel like, and the response is 'like the feeling of a warm bath'. Curious, the coach asks where she feels

that in her body and to describe the feeling so they can check in at the end whether the thought of being with the supervisor brings that same feeling. To gain a sense of the importance of the topic, the coach asks 'How do you feel now as you think of meeting with your supervisor?', to which the response is 'Naked on a street corner'. The internal instinctual response from the coach is wow that's a big difference that feels bigger than an academic discussion. Outwardly, she asks: 'So, what's really going on here?' And the response is: 'I feel too stupid to do a PhD.'

Did you get the felt sense of confession? That is getting to the heart of the matter. Without that exploration, time and energy could be spent thinking of limiting beliefs, power poses, all the foibles that make the supervisor different, but all that would miss the essence of the issue.

My summary reflections

- Establishing a working agreement at the beginning of a coaching session is never wasted time – more a time saver.
- Models can be useful but can hinder if used formulaically.
- Explore connections in multiple subjects before asking to prioritize.
- Each session needs a clear desired outcome.
- Stay with the exploration until there is a felt sense of the topic being real and meaningful for the person and one that they actually want to work on.

Your reflection prompts

- From your experience, what do you now want to add to your conversations with prospective clients about working together?

- What elements of beginning a coaching conversation currently challenge you?

- If you were to think of the beginning of each session as the foundation of your best work, what would you focus on?

- If you aim for clarity through curiosity, how might your coaching sessions begin?

11

Following the thread

Establishing a working agreement is one crucial part of ensuring that those we work with get the outcomes they desire from the conversation, but that is not always a static end position. A term used a lot in coaching is 'dancing in the moment', and this is exactly what we need to do to ensure we are working with what emerges in the conversation. This chapter focuses on the concept of presence in coaching from the perspective of remaining present to what is happening in the conversation. If our aim in coaching is to support the other person to see things from a wider and deeper perspective, it shouldn't surprise us that this can often lead to a change in outcome part way through the session.

We cannot become a slave to the original goal if new insights have the potential to draw the client to a different place. There are a few things that stop coaches from following the thread or 'dancing in the moment':

- Being too obsessed with getting to the original outcome
- Failing to notice an insight or change
- Fearing they will run out of time if the client opens a new thread

- Fearing they will be breaking the rule of not leading the client
- Fearing they will open emotions the client won't be able to deal with

Being too obsessed with getting to the original outcome

By now I hope that you have reflected on your needs in the coaching session and are starting to experiment with loosening your grip on them. It is right to keep the person focused on what they want to achieve, and we can check in when the conversation seems to stray, by, for example, asking: 'And how does that connect to your original thoughts on…?' The alternative can sound something like the following example.

The session starts with the client saying they have been made redundant and would like to use the time to explore how to plan to get a new interim position. The coach works well at evoking awareness – in fact, so well that the client lets out a small laugh, taps her forehead and says: 'what am I thinking, my driver to find another role is financial. I am totally ignoring the fact I have my redundancy package that gives me the time and freedom to really think about what I want to do next.' The coach's response to this emerging insight is: 'So, what's your first step in getting an interim role?'

Failing to notice an insight or change

The example above illustrates two of these pitfalls: the coach's determination to get to action and failing to notice the change in direction. Such a shame when they have obviously done some good work in supporting the client to think differently. Presence is not just about the energy and impact we bring to the session – it is about staying present and focused for any shifts, be they the obvious ones, like a client's expressed change in direction, or slight changes in tone, language, emotion or body language that tell us something has emerged and changed for the client. The client equally may not notice changes in their narrative, subtle or not, so it serves them if the coach notices and acknowledges the shift to provide more information for the client.

Coaching is about evoking awareness and learning. Sir John Whitmore's (2009) simple two-pronged focus for coaching is raising both a person's awareness and their personal responsibility for their choices. Failure to notice that an insight has been reached is such a missed opportunity, not only to make an impact but also to manage the timing of the session, which we will pick up next.

Fearing running out of time if the client opens a new thread

So often as I listen to recordings of coaching sessions in my role as mentor, I hear the missed opportunities for the coach to offer what they notice about this change of subject or new insight that has emerged. Discussing this with the coach in mentoring, they often say they heard it but made a conscious decision to leave it because they were worried about the time left in the session. This is an indicator that the coach has not fully built a working alliance that they have confidence in. If they had, they would be more relaxed knowing this conversation is a partnership, and okay they may be 51% responsible for managing the time, but they are not fully responsible. This 51% might mean the coach is the one responsible for raising the subject, but they and the client can then work out together how they will manage the time.

If the client realizes 10 minutes before the end of the session that they don't want a new interim job, they want to explore what they really want to do next in their career, then, great, it's a different outcome – so how will the coach and client manage this together in the time available? Failing to get to the original goal is only a failure if it remains the goal but they both ignore it once they set it. A changed goal acknowledged and addressed is a success, and new insights bring more clarity. My own approach to noticing new insights is simply to consider three aspects of learning: what does that tell you about the situation, and about yourself, and how do you want to use it? Using our example above, the coach might say: 'That sounds like your thinking has shifted about an interim position. What is your freshest thinking?' 'Anything you notice about yourself?' 'Now you know that, where do you want to focus your attention?' If the goal has changed to something like 'I want to consider my wider options', then the coach and client can agree what would be a useful way to address that in the 10 minutes available.

Fearing breaking the rules by leading the client

This is a particularly sticky rule in coaching. It is such a key element of coach training – it's about the client's agenda, not the coach's, and the coach should never stray into mentoring and using their own experience – that coaches seem terrified of offering the client anything of use from what they notice for fear of leading. There is a difference between offering your observations and leading. Dictionary definitions for 'leading' as an adjective include dominant, most powerful, foremost and front, all of which suggest a position of power and influence, and making decisions for others to follow. Interpreted for coaching, that would be the coach deciding what needs to be discussed, how it will be discussed and what changes should be made. All of this is a far cry from noticing, offering a perspective and leaving it up to the client to do what they want with that information.

Fearing opening emotions the client won't be able to deal with

This is another of the boundary rules drummed into new coaches: stay away from therapy and counselling. It is a useful rule and one that is a hot topic between coaches and therapists, but often a false connection is made between strong emotions emerging in coaching and the need for a therapeutic intervention. There is a myth that we don't deal with emotions in coaching, which is rubbish, especially when life becomes unstable, complex and confusing. You only have to refer to Professor Steve Peters' (2020) simplified book on neuroscience, *The Chimp Paradox*, to know that all information goes to the emotional chimp in our brain first and that this first part it is five times more powerful than the more rational human part of our brain. If the coaching conversation is a container for the client to fully express themselves, it needs to be strong enough to hold the outpourings of what are the totally natural strong emotions of the chimp brain.

This is why it is so important that we do the work on ourselves to become as empty a boat as we can be so that we can sit with the client's emotions without triggering our own chimp to come out and join in. Again, this connects back to partnership and a strong working agreement for how we manage what emerges. It is also the difference between transactional and transformational coaching – the ability to offer that rare gift to another of sitting with them and seeing them fully in their naked vulnerability so that they know they have been fully heard and understood without judgement. If the emotion is less transcendent and is a recurring pattern, then we can revert to the 'what if' plan we agreed at the beginning of our relationship, but that is far more unusual than the hype would suggest. To ignore emotion out of fear means we are not serving our clients, so we need to reflect on that before entering an arena that is steeped in strong emotions.

Following the thread is all about staying present to the other person and the rhythm and flow of the conversation, which will meander. This is a voyage of discovery for the person, and the coach is the lookout and co-pilot noticing the twists and turns and helping the other person stay true to their original destination or making a navigational adjustment when required. Like any exploration, this voyage is all about learning something new or seeing the terrain anew. To partner in this work requires us to release the stranglehold on our need for content to allow attention to be focused on the emerging landscape.

My summary reflections

- Following the thread is a shared activity.
- Learning and insight is key to coaching. Look for it and acknowledge it.
- Outcomes can shift and change. The coach holds the thread to keep a desired outcome in focus.
- Humans are emotional animals. Strong emotions need a safe place to be expressed.
- Sharing experiences is part of partnership.
- Offering insights is not leading, unless I insist on my insights being *the truth*.

Your reflection prompts

- What prevents you from relaxing and noticing what is emerging in the conversation?

- As you experiment with following the thread in your coaching conversations, what do you notice?

- Reflect on times when you have consciously not followed a thread. What stopped you?

12

Coaching the person, not the task

The world of AI is focusing a lot of attention on using biometrics and nonverbal language to interpret the mental state and well-being of humans interacting with it. This field of emotion AI, or affective computing, may be able to detect anxiety, stress, excitement, indifference or any number of emotions and even respond appropriately, but is that really knowing the other person? It is ironic that, according to Brené Brown's (2021) research, as humans, we struggle to identify more than three emotions – happy, sad and mad – and AI is only as intelligent as the humans programming it. A computer cannot empathize, cannot feel along with a person. Being witnessed, heard, seen, felt and understood is a world away from being interpreted, and the former is our aim as coaches.

If coaching is about supporting the person to see themselves more clearly and to notice points of choice and change, we need to see them holistically, not from the view of a problem, an issue or an artificial interpretation of their current mental state. Basic coach training sets up the process of coaching based on the questions 'What do you want?', 'Where are you now?', 'How can you get there?', 'What's your plan?' – all focused on the task. Transcending this approach means balancing the concept of managing the task and putting a focus on the person. What often gets in the way of coaches doing this is their need to be seen to achieve, or their own training as problem-solving individuals – a recurring theme in this move to a more transformational way of working.

I heard a story during one of my undergraduate psychology classes about a famous psychiatrist who emigrated to the United States. I don't recall the name, but the important information was that he was unable to speak or understand English. However, his fame meant he was in demand by troubled American souls, and shortly after he arrived, they flocked to him to tell him their woes. He neither understood their narrative nor offered anything back except a few nods or listening sounds, yet his patients raved about his effectiveness. Whether this is a true story or not, it stuck with me for a couple of reasons. It conveys the power of being listened to with compassion and the power of feeling seen, regardless of our ability to offer solutions. It also demonstrates the element of hope that people invest when seeking support. The more cynical might see this as the placebo effect.

As coaches, if the name of the game is finding solutions to tasks and challenges, we are in big trouble, as AI will do it faster, cheaper and more conveniently. Bringing your humanity to meet the humanity of another is a different story. The focus on finding solutions creates questions about the 'how', 'who' and 'what' of the situation, exploring one solution over another and settling on how to do the preferred one. The focus on the person leads to questions about what stops the person finding their solution, the relationship they have with the situation and what they can learn that will help them not only address this one task but learn something they can apply much more widely.

Everyone has an innate intelligence, and the objective of coaching is to get them back to that wisdom to trust it and help it be their guide – it is the guide that will outlive any coach they work with. Once someone has reconnected with that internal wise counsellor, they will know exactly what to do with whatever challenge they are facing. This is a far more useful service to offer another human being than addressing a task, which often is, quite frankly, stating the blinking obvious. I think about all the people who have offered me the sage advice of 'use a to-do list' to overcome my procrastination issue. I mean, wow, I had never thought of that! It may have been more helpful for any of these well-meaning folk to get to know what stopped me implementing the priorities on my many lists, planning books, apps and diaries. My poor executive function from ADHD means urgency or importance have no impact on me – well, not until I get my 'oh s**t' energy – but interest does. Maybe helping me to connect back to that will allow my wisdom to speak.

My summary reflections

- It is important to balance the focus on both the task and the person.
- It's more important to listen to understand the person than to listen for the key to a solution.
- I can trust in the wisdom and intelligence of the person I am working with to know what they need to know or do.

- The imperfection of my messiness is my unique difference from AI.
- I would rather be connected than right; I don't need to know first or best.

Your reflection prompts

- What prompts you to look for solutions?

- What thoughts come to mind as you consider letting go of your expertise?

- Do you really believe all your clients are up to the task of managing their own life?

- How can you focus your curiosity on the person and away from the content?

13

Listening with purpose

The beauty of listening is that those who are listened to start feeling accepted, start taking their words more seriously and discovering their own true selves.
Henri J.M. Nouwen (2006, reading for 11 March)

A key skill we are encouraged to enhance as coaches is that of listening. Of course, it is a basic life skill that those of us blessed with hearing use constantly. Many training schools use one or other model of listening scale to differentiate between the different levels of listening. One example is Otto Scharmer's (2008) four levels of listening: downloading, factual listening, empathic listening and generative listening. Most models recognize there is an incremental increase from a basic level of distracted listening through to empathic listening and, ultimately, a more global form of listening – listening beyond what is being said.

While coaches generally put a lot of effort into listening well, there are still common areas of challenge they can face in the first half of coaching, such as:

- Focusing on identifying 'the problem'
- Getting caught in the content
- Needing to be seen to be listening

Henri Nouwen (2006) refers to listening as a kind of spiritual hospitality, and as we see from the quote that opens this chapter, truly listening to someone has the power to help them see themselves fully. This one concept puts the focus of the reason for listening clearly into perspective: listening is for the other person to hear and know themselves, not for the coach to gather information. That may sound like a truism, but let that sink in. This circles back to the idea of looking into the client's world with curiosity on behalf of them, not for our own benefit. We are asking in service of the client's awareness.

If our listening attention is focused on seeking the problem, we cannot offer this level of hospitality, nor can we notice the real story beneath the surface. We are all so much more than any problem we may have in the moment – they will pass. What is more useful is to understand more about how we view problems and see them in relation to who we are. The content is just one strand of the story, and it is transient. Psychological experiments have shown the malleability of memory. We don't accurately record and report memories exactly as they happened (Loftus and Palmer, 1974). What is more interesting is how the person interprets the content and what meaning they derive from it. We demonstrate our listening through much more than parroting back summaries of what we have heard.

In his study of effective outcomes in counselling, Robert Carkhuff (1969) identified six dimensions that can help us to consider our listening in coaching: respect, genuineness, empathy, concreteness, confrontation and immediacy. All of these apply to this transcendent approach to coaching. Notice the similarities to Carl Rogers' necessary and sufficient conditions, discussed in Chapter 3. In Table 3, I offer some of my interpretations of Carkhuff's work in relation to coaching and hope I do not distort his original meaning too much.

Table 3: My interpretation of Carkhuff's dimensions

Dimension	My Interpretation
Respect	Acknowledging the person as whole, resourceful and unique Honouring the person's lived experience and identity without making assumptions
Genuineness	Being fully present just as you are, without trying to be anything else or look good Being another messy human
Empathy	Viewing the world through another's perspective Noticing and understanding the feelings and emotions of another
Concreteness	Supporting another to avoid vagueness and bringing clarity and focus to the conversation
Confrontation	Noticing incongruencies, beliefs, behaviours or energy shifts in oneself and others and having the courage to respectfully draw them into view
Immediacy	Being aware of what is being created in the relationship in the moment

These dimensions highlight the intimate link between listening and intervening to support the client to move forward or bring about change. This purposeful listening will always transcend what AI can bring to coaching. AI cannot empathize, nor can it bring the humanity of another living being and the energy that is created between two people. Listening is the foundational tool for building a presence that means the other person knows they have been seen, heard and understood, not only through their words but through their whole being.

The first three of these dimensions are all about who the coach is and the sense of presence they bring to their listening, and the last three are what they do with that listening – the 'what' they are listening for. We have covered the first three in discussing how a coach becomes an empty boat, being aware of their own triggers and managing them, bringing curiosity to understand and feel, as much as another person can, what it is like to live in another's world and to recognize the other's perspective. Listening from this grounding, attention can be focused on the rhythm, pace and sound of the conversation. Specific words may seem to hold power or provoke deeper questions.

We all express ourselves differently – some of us with clarity and logic, some more poetically through metaphors or expressive language. All can be symbols to a greater truth that we can listen out for and work with. If we assume that there is a deeper truth to our communication, then the words or images we use are far from accidental, even if we are consciously unaware as we speak them. Listening with purpose means the coach is focused on not just the content but how we choose to share it.

Harry Potter fans will be familiar with the portkey, an enchanted object that can take anyone touching it to just the right location. In a coaching conversation, the coach focusing their attention on how something is said more than on the details will notice certain words that stand out. Just as a portkey can be an everyday object like an old boot, in a non-coaching conversation, these everyday words may not raise suspicion, but to the coaching wizard they can be the portal to just the place for exploration. It may be the word itself that creates curiosity, or it may be the way it is said, the emphasis or incongruence. Reflecting just the word or the energy expressed can open new vistas while respecting the person's view of their world.

Similarly, when someone chooses imagery or similes in their conversation, we can attend to that, exploring the images or even sharing ones that occur to us from the language used to communicate an experience or situation. There seems to be a rule in coaching that we always work with the client's metaphors and do not introduce our own. It is a rule I often transcend. That doesn't mean I ignore the metaphor of the other person – I love to work with their metaphors. But if they have not introduced one and one comes to mind for me, I will share it, with permission. Sometimes people love them and make them their own; sometimes the metaphor doesn't land with them and we move on. Any metaphor that I might introduce has only come from what I have heard and what that has conjured up for me, so it's only useful if it helps in expanding the client's awareness.

Listening with respect

Respect for the person and their life, beliefs and autonomy permeates through all our coaching and in each dimension of listening. We can demonstrate this respect by honouring the person's perspective, giving them space and time to speak at their own pace and in their own time. As we explored earlier, this is about valuing the person's lived experience and the unique impact situations have on them rather than making assumptions based on our own.

Listening with genuineness and empathy

Our own needs, drivers and narratives can really take us away from bringing our own authentic self to listening. I know I used to have the naive belief that I needed to be all sorted before I could coach anyone else – that was before I recognized that was never going to happen. It helped for me to think about the kind of person that I would be comfortable sharing the shadowy side of myself with, and it certainly wouldn't be a fully together, perfectly sorted and coiffured coach or a coach who tells me I just need to think positively or follow the route they did to become perfect. I want someone who gives me the hope – hope that if this person has found a way to self-acceptance, then so can I.

Genuineness is the same as one of Carl Rogers' (1957) six necessary and sufficient conditions: congruence, described as being authentic genuine and present. This isn't something that can be feigned. We have a greater chance of being able to listen for the other person's feelings and world-view with compassion if we have let go of the stranglehold of our own. It's no good just seeing and feeling the life and emotions of others and keeping it to yourself; the person needs to know they have been seen, heard and felt. This is conveyed in your genuine felt response, from one human to another, to what you are hearing. I have heard so many coaching conversations that fail to do this, as if being in the professional role means an objective stance. A genuine response may be as simple as 'that sounds tough', but it conveys that depth of connection.

Listening for clarity: concreteness

The first time I recognized I was being truly listened to, it was uncomfortable. I am sure I must have been listened to before, as I was well into my forties, but it struck me forcefully on this occasion. I knew I was being listened to because the questions that were generated from my meandering were so specific and targeted. This wasn't a coaching conversation, but one with a work colleague, Sarah. Someone who was trained as a researcher and scientist. We were planning some work together, and I was bringing what I often do to these sorts of conversations – creative and innovative solutions that are great starting points but never thought-through. Sarah's questions made me uncomfortable; I wanted to ask her not to listen to me as I was just saying the first thing that came into my head, but her genuine support and curiosity helped me to relax and think about how to implement, or not, these initial ideas.

This is the listening required in coaching. The ability to support someone to go from vague thoughts and generalizations to clarity and understanding. As Henri Nouwen suggests in the quote from earlier, the other person can take their own words seriously and perhaps discover their true feelings about something or their true desires. We add value by listening for the vagueness and seeking clarity.

Jiminy Cricket listening: confrontation

Confrontation can be a troublesome word when attached to coaching. Those familiar with the intervention styles in the work of John Heron (1975) will recognize the *confrontative* style for leaders as one of the six interventions for effectiveness. The word infers aggression at worst and, at best, this idea of challenge so often used in coaching. Like Clynes' (1977) sentic states, which we explored in Chapter 3, this is more about meeting the need of the other person at a specific time. Done with respect and care, this can transform thinking. Jiminy Cricket was Pinocchio's conscience in the well-known story by Carlo Collodi – this role is a bit of a stretch for a coach, but being able to notice and check in on any discrepancies in beliefs, thoughts or actions can be a useful aide to the person's thinking and exploration of options. Blakey and Day (2012) refer to the role of the coach in challenging thinking as ensuring that the person making decisions that affect others has really thought about the impact of their actions on themselves and those around them. A little like Jiminy's role as the conscience.

'In the moment' listening: immediacy

Listening is not restricted to listening to the other person, but is also about listening to oneself and what is emerging between you and the other person. If we think about everything that occurs in the coaching conversation and relationship as data that can help evoke awareness in the client, what we feel can add to that data. Like confrontation, immediacy can only work in a strong trusting relationship and if it has been agreed when establishing the working alliance. If a coach notices they are becoming impatient with the lack of forward movement in a session, or they sense that everything is going in circles, that can be useful data to share with the client. They should of course be respectful and sensitive when sharing this.

It may seem simple to have the courage to share a sense of 'stuckness', but what if you are feeling bored by the person you are coaching, you are overcome by sleepiness in their company or you notice a sense of disbelief in response to something the client is sharing? How ready would you be to share that? Blurting out everything we feel can induce shame and convey judgement to the other person, so we need to be sure that what we want to share is in service of the client and not just our own impatience, tiredness or some emotion. Discerning the difference is the skill. One way that may help as you notice whatever you are experiencing is to consider whether this is this something unusual for you. For example, it is highly unusual for me to feel impatient with a client, so it is curious if I do, and if it continues through the session I might raise it gently, owning my own feelings without attributing them to anything or anyone else. In the same way as offering a feeling of being stuck, I might say: 'I am noticing a sense of impatience in myself. How are you feeling?' It is all down to experimentation and partnership.

Silence and reflection

We all know that in coaching we expect the client to speak far more than the coach and that listening and asking questions are two key skills in the process. What seems less prevalent in less experienced coaches is an appreciation of the usefulness of silence and reflection time. The idea of coaching as dancing in the moment has already been touched on, as has the rhythm of the conversation. These ideas could be expanded to consider the musicality of coaching. Considering listening and questions without this backdrop can lead to something that sounds like an interview – as soon as the person being coached answers one question, another is posed. The questions may be useful, but without time and space for reflection, their power is lost. The questions need time to do their work.

In music, the space between the notes is just as important as the notes themselves. Similarly, coaching happens in the space between the words. That is where reflection can happen. Bringing art to the science of coaching means getting comfortable with silence and being able to sit alongside someone using that space to reflect without feeling the need to fill those precious gaps. The more artful the coach, the less they need to speak. Even at those points where the other person may say they don't know or ask a rhetorical question, a skilled coach can let the discomfort just be and let silence do its work.

Silence is a way of being rather than a specific act. There are times when, as a mentor, I listen to coaching recordings and there is silence, but it somehow sounds forced or loaded, often when the coach is purposefully using silence as a tool. It is hard to describe, but the quality of the silence sounds different. There is something beyond the act of silence that is conveyed in the being of the coach, the encouragement in a glance or the expectation in the breathing space that produces deep focused attention. It is the slowing down, allowing for thinking to emerge in the space between the words. Of course, this thinking time is for the person being coached, not for the coach to think of their next question – that sort of silence can create an awkwardness.

It can be a challenge to stay silent if you are not used to it and especially if you are focused on proving your worth as a coach. It is so seductive to fall straight into offering thoughts when someone says: 'I don't know. What do you think?' It is so much harder to stay silent and let them do the work.

Listening is not a passive act in coaching, and our listening and attention is put to far better service for our clients if the focus is on the person behind the narrative, not the narrative itself. That focus might be on the energy shifts in the narrative, the specific words or phrases, the tone and the pace – all contribute to seeing the world through the eyes of the client. We listen in coaching in order to support the other person to broaden and deepen their awareness. What we observe and hear helps us to respond in a way that aides that, whether that be with a question, an observation or simply silence, everything is in service of the client understanding themselves and their situation more.

My summary reflections

- Listening involves the whole of me, not just my ears.
- Listening is the foundation of presence and the source of curious questions.
- Listening is hospitality.
- There may be silence in the conversation, but in our heads, sparks are flying.

Your reflection prompts

- If your coaching conversations were put to music, what would the tune be?

- How do you respond to silence?

- What dimension of your listening could do with a tune-up?

14

If you are not evoking awareness, you might as well give up

In 1998, the International Coaching Federation developed their core coaching competency framework. They revised this model in 2019, reducing the core competencies from 11 to 8. One of the most significant changes was the removal of 'powerful questions' as a discreet competency and its replacement with a more relevant skill of 'evoking awareness'. This was a positive change to include a range of interventions that do not rely solely on questions. Still, there seems to be a hangover of the concept of the powerful question as some sort of magical tool in the coach's toolbox, leading to issues for the coach, such as:

- Long, convoluted questions
- Use of standard coaching questions
- Failure to ask the most obvious question
- The sheepdog approach to questions

Let's start by blasting the myth of the powerful question. You don't need to find the powerful question; the question will find you. And when it does, it may not sound powerful or even grammatically correct, but if you are transcending the rules and asking what comes to mind from what you hear, it will do the job. Coach education and competency frameworks have done a real disservice to coaches by introducing this notion of the powerful question. At the time of writing, a search on Amazon for 'powerful questions for coaches' brings up 90 books. Opening that out to 'powerful questions' brings forth 903, but reducing it to just 'questions' brings results for around 50,000 books. It seems there is quite an industry built around the concept that we can pre-prepare questions for future conversations.

Generally, we ask questions because we are seeking an answer, but in coaching, we use them differently. Questions are being asked so the person being questioned can hear the answer and see things from a potentially different perspective. Trying to stay within the rules of asking powerful questions can lead coaches to focus attention on their own performance. Thinking energy can be expended searching for a clever question, chasing after that elusive 'aha' moment for the client that assures the coach they are good enough. Relying on a list of powerful questions can mean the coach adapts tried and tested ones that have little or no real connection to what the other person has said. One such question that is bandied around the coaching profession, and is often pulled out of the bag if a client ever says 'I don't know', is: 'If you did know, what would you say/do?' Even as a pacifist, I would get the urge to lash out if my coach asked that.

Long, convoluted questions

A question that has the power to evoke insight in another person can be one word or a simple repetition of a word used by the client with a question intonation. It doesn't always sound clever, but it is an authentic response to what has been heard. This is why I am confident in saying you don't need to seek a question – it will find you. It will be your response to listening with curiosity that will bring a question to mind. Of course, your experience and courage will influence whether you use that first uncensored question. A trap that can catch a coach out is taking an emerging question and prettying it up to make it less direct and more acceptable in their view. The problem with this is that the power of the original question is lost in a sea of words.

We can get caught up in adding a narrative before posing a question to justify why we are asking it or to guarantee that the person understands what we are asking. Often this confuses and stops any real revelation. There will be times that someone totally misconstrues the question we pose, but that can be the most enlightening experience for them, as they will answer the question they thought they heard. When all is said and done, surely that is more important than getting a precise interpretation of what we thought would be useful.

The sheepdog approach to questions

I was once walking with friends in the Yorkshire Dales when we saw what looked like a choreographed dance on a hillside way above us. A shepherdess on a quad bike was working her sheepdog to corral the sheep into a pen. The movement between the woman and the animals flowed elegantly, a little like the dance of a coaching conversation. We were entranced and continued to climb towards this incidental display. As we got closer, the magic of the image was shattered as we heard her shouting at the dog 'For f**k's sake, get around back' and other expletive-rich instructions, rather than the traditional whistle-calls. This reminded me so much of how some coaches work so hard to corral their clients to see something or get to a conclusion that they have already seen. Far from the elegant dance of coaching that works in response to the clients thinking, this type of questioning is jarring, leading and has a clear intention. The questions include: 'Have you thought of…?' or 'Could you perhaps…?' If you have an idea or thought, it is far better to own it, share it and know it's only your truth and that it may not be useful, so be prepared to let it go rather than shepherd the client to see the situation as you do.

Awareness is more than questions

Evoking awareness is about so much more than questions. The intent is to support the client to review their life, beliefs, emotions, assumptions and behaviours from different perspectives to gain fresh insight that they can apply to their enquiry. It is not always a question that achieves this; it can be silence and the sense of acceptance from another that allows the person to relax and let insights emerge. It can come through sharing metaphors or acknowledging feelings, observations and creativity. Whatever way awareness is evoked, it is key to coaching. Remember, if the client has not learnt anything or seen anything differently, what real value have we added?

There is an intimate link between listening and evoking awareness, and this is why I find Carkhuff's (1969) framework for therapeutic conversations, explored in Chapter 13, so helpful, particularly the elements of concreteness, confrontation and immediacy. Without these three elements, coaching can sound a little too much like a conversation with a friend – comforting and supportive, but nothing necessarily changes. Some coaches find this challenging aspect of coaching the most difficult to apply, fearing making the client uncomfortable. Coaching is not about keeping people comfortable; in fact, the intent is entirely the opposite. I often steal a phrase I heard Michael Neill use once: 'coaching is not meant to comfort the afflicted but to afflict the comfortable'. All change is uncomfortable; hence we co-create a *brave* space with our clients where they can face that discomfort and grow.

From awareness to action

A key element of coaching is the forward movement. We are working with clients to apply their new thinking to their behaviour, so we need to do something with the raised awareness.

When someone gets to the point of knowing, seeing or feeling something differently, they are at the point of choice. They have agency; they can do nothing if they so choose – that is still a choice. Coaching is not just for one problem – it's for life. At any point of awareness, there is an opportunity for the person to learn something new about themselves or the situation. At this point they can decide how they want to apply that learning to the situation they are exploring and also how to extend it to their life as whole.

A lovely example from my coaching is of a young man who wanted to be a more confident leader. Through our coaching conversation, he realized that even if he didn't have this thing he recognized as confidence, he always had the courage to have a go. Taking time to reflect on that insight and explore what it meant for the situation and his life generally, he chose to find ways to remind himself that he had courage that gave him the confidence to do whatever his leadership role called on him to do. His plan for future wobbles of confidence? He now has a picture of the lion from *The Wizard of Oz* on his desk that he can glance at as a reminder that even if he wasn't feeling confident, he had the courage to do things anyway.

My summary reflections

- If clients don't know, feel or see something from a different perspective at the end of a session, or if they have not at least been prompted to reflect further on something, they haven't been coached.
- Listening and evoking awareness are intimately linked.
- Powerful questions emerge from deep presence and listening. They can't be planned.
- Awareness comes from more than questions.
- Comfort is not the aim – new thinking is.
- Choice and personal agency mean awareness can be transformed into action.

Your reflection prompts

- How can you improve your ability to notice insights and learning?

- In what ways do you self-censor your interventions?

- What happens to you when you notice your client is uncomfortable?

- What is your reaction to choice?

15

Not everyone is looking for action

Foundational coach training encourages coaches to work towards a clearly defined and measurable goal or a well packaged to-do list. Touching another human soul doesn't always come with a SMART (specific, measurable, achievable, relevant and time-bound) goal. Transcending this SMART goal rule does not mean abandoning the idea of clear and well-defined outcomes, but rather reflects a more flexible approach to what is meaningful and identifiable for the person. Really great coaching relies on the 'bookends' being clear – a beginning linked to the end – while allowing for detours along the way. However, coaching may not always require an action plan.

Rarely do any of us get the time to reflect and ponder on life and our own responses to it. This can be even more pronounced in the workplace. There is a comical notion that we can separate out work and home, achieving a work-life balance. As a working mother and now as a grandmother with extended family and all its ups and downs, I have never achieved this mystical balance. I just tottered precariously close to the precipice, navigating barriers and diving into opportunities as they arose, surviving by the skin of my teeth. One thing that would have been a beautiful luxury for me would have been the time to reflect, to ponder on what was important to me and my family and how I wanted to be in the middle of the chaos, to consider options rather than jumping on the next best thing. In other words, it would have helped to engage in coaching as a coachee much earlier in my life.

Many people have similar complex and busy lives to the one I had with four children and a high-pressure job, and they really want their coaching to be a time of reflection and space to breathe, not a time to hit goals and achieve. Reflection and clear outcomes are not mutually exclusive. Like the intimate link between listening and evoking awareness, the ending of a coaching conversation is based on the clarity of the outcome identified at the beginning. Clarity is even more important when the client says they want to spend their time thinking about where they are or reflecting on what is happening in their life/work/family. Those times, it is less about a task-oriented outcome and more about deep reflection. It can be tempting to take that at face value and get started on reflecting, but then how do you know what will make a difference?

If the intention of coaching is to know oneself and the situation more intimately, a key part of the ending must be to check in on what has been discovered or realized that was not in awareness at the start of the session. If coaching has done its job, the person being coached has changed in some way – they know or feel something differently, and they may be challenging long-held beliefs. A well-thought-out ending will help them to consolidate that learning and start to integrate the new thinking into their lives. A coach who is less concerned with an action plan and more concerned with helping the person transcend the one presenting issue can help them do that.

It is quite usual for someone who has been coached to feel a sense of empowerment and hope at the end of a session, regardless of the quality of the coaching. If someone has been listened to and has had the opportunity to unburden themselves, there will be relief, but how long does that last? I recall one person I coached many years ago who spent the whole of our session unburdening themselves about all the wrongdoings of fellow executive team members and offering thoughts on how they could all improve. They left the session delighted that it was all 'off their chest'. I reflected on the session knowing that this person had no new thinking as they left.

At the start of our next session, I encouraged us both to reflect on the person having said they had found it really useful. That could have been a signal to continue, but I checked in on what was different other than the person feeling better. What was new or different about their learning? That's when the penny dropped for them: nothing. Following this realization, we were able to create a partnership for them to get the best out of the session. We agreed they would take 10 minutes to download at the beginning and then we would get to the real work. We can be lulled into a false service for the client if we decide, or they tell us, they just really need to get something off their chest. Of course, there is a place for that, but they already know all of the ins and outs of the story, and you don't need to. So, at least get an agreement on what they want to get from the download and how they will know they got it.

Ending well, with or without an action plan

Ending well begins with starting well, which we have discussed, but it is worth repeating here: make sure you know what will make the time in conversation worthwhile, even if it happens to be a space for reflection, not action. For example, if someone wants to reflect on an experience or incident to understand it a little more, what will they know, feel or have that is useful at the end of the reflection? How will they know they have that? What makes it important for them to understand that? What is the 'ouch' that keeps it on their mind? If you both start the conversation with this in mind, you have a thread to track your way through the reflections, and you can check in on what the person has learnt and where that leads them next.

Timing

Great coaching leaves time for a smooth descent to the end rather than a crash landing. How many times have you been filled with anxiety while watching the clock and wondering how to get finished on time? Or perhaps you have suddenly recognized you have five minutes or less left and the session is nowhere near a conclusion? If you keep running out of time, maybe you regularly suggest you add a little more time to the sessions. All this is part of the learning process and nothing unusual, but you can find your way to managing the time so that the ending feels elegant and smooth. This is a fundamental task for the coach: managing the process.

I used to feel I had to secretly manage the time, surreptitiously looking at the clock that was strategically placed behind the client so that I could look without being seen to check it. I forgot all of that when I started to see the relationship as a partnership where, although I was ultimately managing the time on behalf of the client so that they were free to think, we would both be responsible for using the time well. We can use time positively as we draw towards the final 10 or 15 minutes of a session, checking in with something like: 'As we come to our final 15 minutes, what would be most useful for you to consider?' Even if, at this point, someone has a profound insight or hits an emotional curveball, it can still be managed within the agreed time frame if considered in partnership. 'That sounds significant. How would you like to use the time we have to work with it?'

Putting the new thinking to work

The neurolinguistic programming concept of a well-formed outcome is useful here. As we know from research by McKenna and Davis (2009) into the effective elements of therapy, one of the major indicators of success is external factors, things that happen outside of the coaching. It is useful to remember that 40% of the success of coaching is not down to the coach at all (that keeps our ego in check) but to the person's systems, networks and support as well as the person themselves. We can use this knowledge to support the person to leverage all the support they can from their networks to overcome any barriers in the system.

This is where the concreteness in our listening is useful, as it helps the person consolidate their learning, plan to implement it and build the motivation to make it happen. Whether it is to change some behaviour, complete a certain task or just experiment with a new thought or belief, there can be a concrete application. It could be as simple as having a picture as a reminder, like the one of the lion in *The Wizard of Oz* (see Chapter 14), an anchoring thought or something like an action plan to have that difficult conversation on Tuesday, but making it concrete will mean there is a better chance it will materialize.

Keeping accountability where it belongs

A question I get asked a lot is how do I make sure clients complete what they have agreed to complete, and should I check in at the next session? These questions tell me much more about the coach than anyone they are working with. It suggests the coach is far too invested in the outcome and taking on too much responsibility. It is so easily done. I recall that at the beginning of my coaching career, I worked so hard and took far too much responsibility. Luckily, my ADHD means I can quickly lose interest in doing routine things like follow-up notes, and this fell into that category. It was such a liberation when I realized that I am not accountable for the success of my client, and they are not accountable for me to complete actions. That creates such a power differential – one I am very uncomfortable with.

On the question of asking about the actions at the next session, of course that is up to you. I don't, because I don't want to create a relationship where the other person is either completing tasks to please me or afraid to come back if they fail. If someone comes and sheepishly tells me they did nothing they said they were going to do, my only response is: 'Okay, so what did you learn?' If I start to be the arbiter of whether someone fails or succeeds, I am both taking away their learning and taking the credit for their success.

Checking on past agreed actions is also looking backwards, rather than the forward-looking approach we take in coaching. Remember, most of life happens between the sessions. Life will have moved on, and situations change. If recounting past actions is important, the client will bring it up – we don't need to.

Celebrating endings

Endings are interesting things, and we all have our personal relationship with endings. I have a dear friend who is a nightmare to leave a party with. She loves to say a long and personal goodbye to everyone. I, on the other hand, prefer an Irish exit. This is an unfair stereotype of my ancestors, because the Irish are known for their generous hospitality, but nevertheless the Irish exit is a term for leaving a party without telling anyone. There is a sense of embarrassment for me in the goodbyes, so I want to get it over with as quickly as possible or totally avoid it. It is not a great way to end a coaching session or relationship, so it is something I have reflected and worked on. It is useful for coaches to reflect on their own relationship with endings and how this has the potential to impact their work.

Ending a coaching session and relationship well holds all the forward plans but there is also a place for recognizing how far the person has come and all that they have achieved. It is all too easy to rush past the work and struggle the person has gone through to get to their current position, but recognizing and acknowledging this can help them see that they can call on the attributes they used in any future endeavour. It also ensures that the person takes the credit for positive outcomes themself rather than attributing it to the coach.

Unplanned endings

We can work on endings right from the beginning, yet there are still times when coaching clients just go off radar – without warning, they are no longer in communication. If this hasn't happened to you yet, there is a strong chance it will in future. Some codes of ethics set out that this should be a clear right for the client, a sort of 'no-blame divorce' with no requirement to give a reason for terminating the coaching. Ensuring this is the case for the client is great, but it leaves the coach with questions that they may not get answers to and can trigger all sorts of self-judgement and knocks to the confidence.

This happened to me several years ago, and I spiralled straight to self-recrimination, questioning my abilities as a coach. There was potentially something for me to learn from the work we had been engaged in, but of course I cannot be sure, because I never found out. That is the difficult part for coaches – not knowing why the person disengaged. I explored the experience with my supervisor to understand my reaction to the disengagement and my thoughts on what could have been the catalyst, and I adapted how I set up and planned for unplanned endings.

Planning for the possibility of disengagement takes a lot of the embarrassment and shame out of the experience for coach and client. We know from systemic thinking that relationships need good endings or there will be hangovers going into new relationships. In my case, I made many attempts to re-engage with the person via email, to no avail. Then, months later, I happened to be walking down a long, empty corridor at their workplace and from afar I spotted them walking towards me. I could almost hear the tune from *The Good, The Bad and the Ugly* playing as we walked towards each other, each visibly embarrassed and rehearsing our greeting. We did the usual 'oh we must catch up', both knowing that wasn't going to happen. A poor ending meant things were left unsaid, unresolved.

I didn't want to put myself or anyone else through that again, so I now plan for these endings by talking about the possibility when we are agreeing how to work together and exploring the 'what ifs'. This normalizes that it happens sometimes, it's okay and they don't need to give a reason, but it sets the backdrop for us to be able to have conversations if there is anything that is not working for the client. I am also much more willing to raise anything I notice in the relationship or session that could affect our connection, using the immediacy highlighted in Carkhuff's six dimensions.

My summary reflections

- Endings need to be planned for and worked towards from the beginning.
- Action plans and to-do lists are not a requirement, but a clear outcome is.
- An outcome could be a new understanding, learning or perspective.

- There is no 'we' at the ending stage of coaching – this is all down to the client.
- Like each coaching session, the ending of the relationship needs to be planned for.
- Coaching is about learning, throughout the sessions and at the end, and time is needed to consolidate new thinking.

Your reflection prompts

- What is your experience so far of endings in the coaching relationship?

- Thinking of the endings of your coaching sessions as a landing, how elegant are they?

- What could you experiment with to make them smooth landings?

16

Developing professional and ethical maturity

Life is a balance between holding on and letting go.

Rumi

Throughout this book, there have been explicit and implicit references to the concept of getting familiar with not knowing, letting go of our need for certainty. Developing ethical maturity relies on us grasping that concept and living it. I say living it because ethics is for life, not just for coaching. Who we are ethically will undoubtedly show up in our coaching relationships and behaviours. The only certainty in ethical coaching is that there will be uncertainty, no simple right or wrong guide, so as coaches we need to build our maturity in dealing with dilemmas as they arise. The paradox of remaining ethical is that balance between surrendering to not knowing while taking the best action in the moment.

Yes, we have the 'rules' of coaching and the ethical codes of whichever professional bodies we belong to, but ethical practice transcends the rules. The conundrums we encounter as coaches are as vast and varied as the people we coach, if we are awake to them. Sadly, there are many coaches operating without reference to any code of ethics, many not seeing the value of investing in supervision or even recognizing the need for vigilance. Codes of ethics and professional practice simply offer the basics as a guide.

Far from being deliberately careless when working with others in coaching, I am sure many of us believe we know what is right and wrong and are sure of our values and confident of identifying when we are close to a potential problem. Well, that's how we delude ourselves anyway. Thinking about your life outside of coaching, can you recall a time when you have known there was a right path in some situation or other and taken the exact opposite? How did you justify your decision? I can certainly think of many occasions when I have, and I could give a justification worthy of a defence lawyer. Our real ethical maturity shows up in how we justify the decisions we make.

Carroll and Shaw (2013, p. 30) define 'ethical maturity' as:

the reflective, rational, emotional and intuitive capacity to decide actions are right and wrong, or good and better; the resilience and courage to implement those decisions; the willingness to be accountable for ethical decisions made (publicly or privately) and, the ability to learn from and live with the experience.

There is so much wisdom to unpick in this definition – the recognition that there may not be right or wrong options or decisions, just some potentially better ones, and that we arrive at them through more than rational thinking. The shift that makes the difference is having the moral courage to take accountability to implement those decisions and be at peace when we have.

To be aware of ethical dilemmas and address them, we need to have our eyes opened to the potential of their existence.

Education is the starting place to gain an ethical sensitivity, but Smith et al. (2023) identify the problem with relying on coach education providers. When they reviewed programmes, it seemed ethics was often the preserve of the more advanced programmes, not a fundamental element of a lot of coach training. In university settings, they claim only 40% of programmes accredited by professional bodies explicitly referenced ethics was part of the programme. My experience of my first coach training was that ethics was not really covered in any depth, and although that was over 20 years ago, and coaching was a much more transactional engagement at that time, ethical issues still arose.

As Carroll and Shaw (2013, p. 39) highlight, we don't start from a position of ethical maturity – we grow into it. If coach education is not starting that growth, how do coaches begin to build that muscle? Personal reflection is one approach, but we can only go as far as our own understanding, experience and learning can take us; we need support to challenge us to think beyond our current capacity. In a study by Hawkins and Turner (2017), a significant number of coaches who were not in professional supervision said they either engaged in their own self-reflection or in peer supervision – both useful, but does that help growth?

Supervision from someone further on the journey of growth as a coach is one way we can have space to do that, and more coaches are engaging in this reflective practice as the profession itself matures. In 2006, according to the research by Hawkins and Turner (2017), although 86% of coaches thought it was important for them to receive supervision, only 44% of them actually did. In a follow-up survey in 2014, over 92% received supervision. These may well be the more conscientious coaches, and as we all know there are many coaches operating with only the basic training who may not even think of reflection.

To transcend the rules wisely when we are all messy human beings muddling our way through life, we need a solid ground to stand on. The premise of this book is that we need to lean on our own understanding, our own wisdom, and to do that we need to spend time getting to know ourselves, our strengths and our weaknesses. When we come to the coaching relationship, we bring all our histories, learning, triggers, biases and human frailty, and all that we are will influence the ethical decisions we make. Reflection and supervision can help us explore this messiness we are bringing to coaching and navigate a way through it. A supervisor can help us to explore our options and actions in ethical dilemmas, stretch our thinking, support us to stay 'fit to practise' and help us learn and grow long after our coach training.

Ethical action often involves difficult conversations, which Carroll and Shaw acknowledge in their definition when they speak of 'resilience and courage' to implement decisions. We may know what needs to be said or done in a given situation but fail to act for a variety of reasons. If we have any responsibility in the coaching relationship, it is in the realm of ensuring we are behaving responsibly and professionally and that we can confidently defend our decisions. This responsibility has to come above our need to win or keep business, be liked or fit in. Yes, it is difficult to raise sensitive issues or challenge potentially harmful behaviours or decisions but much harder to live with the consequences of doing nothing.

Carroll and Shaw (2013) identify six components of ethical maturity: sensitivity, discernment, implementation, conversation, peace and growth. Their book *Ethical Maturity in the Helping Professions* explores each of these in detail, offering developmental approaches to building this muscle. My intention is merely to encourage you to be aware that transcending the rules requires you to develop this maturity to ultimately draw on your wisdom and the wisdom of others to support you to work in a way that makes you confident that you can justify your actions.

We can keep this balance of holding on and letting go more easily if we establish a practice of reflection, carving out space to connect with our inner wisdom. I am often reminded of the importance of this time of taking oneself away from the madness of first-stage-of-life thinking and dropping into just being and letting wisdom surface. The mind can be like a jar of murky water taken from a pond. If we wanted to clean it, there are a few ways we could try. My ADHD brain would want to go to action by boiling, filtering out whatever bits I wanted to remove. But there is another option: let it sit, settle and clear. I'm not sure I would want to drink it – still, it would be clearer, and that is my point. When we are faced with an ethical dilemma, we can rush about looking at what the rules say, seeking support, playing out the various options – all really good and necessary steps. But what if we could just sit with the question first and let it settle, then see what wisdom has to tell us.

My summary reflections

- The more aware I become, the more I see ethical choice points.
- I know I am an ethical person, and I also know I sometimes behave unethically.
- There are experienced coaches in the profession who I can work with and learn from.
- There are no definite answers, only decisions I have come to after careful consideration – my best in the moment – and when I allow my wisdom to speak, I get a sense of what is best.
- I can't know if there was a better decision, as I didn't make it, so I need to be comfortable with knowing I did the best with what I knew at the time.

Your reflection prompts

- What can influence you to act in a way that does not align with your own ethical code?

- When you have acted in a way that was not strictly ethical, how did you justify this to yourself?

- What process to you have for working through ethical dilemmas?

17

The end of the beginning

There is so much to learn in this profession of ours, and it is still early days. More and more coaches are joining the profession, and new technologies are stretching and challenging the way we work. Not so many years ago, the majority of coaching was either face to face or via telephone. The pandemic quickly got all of us familiar with online conferencing and now most of my coaching, mentoring and supervision is conducted that way and meeting for sessions in workplaces and hotels is a special treat for me. This rapid change over the last few years and the changes in the 30 or so years before that since coaching became more popularized mean we cannot hold onto the view that we are a young profession. We are at least teenagers now and we need to build eldership into the family.

Research to inform the practice of coaching has been increasing and building the body of knowledge over the last 20 years. We now have much more evidence-based practices and approaches to coaching and coach education. The programmes I have led and still teach on are totally different to the first coach education I did when I joined the profession. Psychological approaches to behaviour change are now integral to the development of coaching, and developments in neuroscience are adding knowledge to the practice of coaching constantly. All this growth and development makes this an exciting time to be working in the field.

As we learn more, the rules will naturally stretch and change, as they should to accommodate fresh understanding. Receiving my very late ADHD diagnosis and working and talking with other people with neurodiverse profiles has caused me to question some of the sacred 'truths' we have accepted in our development as coaches. I recognize the value of having a framework built on evidence that can offer us the general guide-rails for a coaching relationship and conversation, but I cannot accept them as unchallengeable. We need experienced coaches to take on the mantle of eldership to bring wisdom and soul into the science of coaching.

There are so many wise coaches around – not all of them have the badges, books, profiles and awards that flaunt that wisdom, but they are there for us to learn from and grow with. Some are not even coaches. I encourage you to spread your wings in your quest to become the coach you were always meant to be and call on your courage to challenge rules that are not serving the people you work with, because ultimately that is what we are all trying to do. There is wisdom and truth in more than coaching books. Anyone who has worked with me will know that I often sprinkle thoughts from children's films, poems, spirituality and holy books in with psychology and silly life experiences.

My challenge to you is: learn the rules of coaching and learn them well so that you can transcend them safely and in service of your clients. There is a time for learning the foundations to build your practice on, but keep learning and growing. There is a trend for working towards getting the badges of accreditation, and I have been on that trend, working through the various credential levels to give me the assurance I am good enough. They go some way to do that, but from my experience, I would urge you not to hang all your worth on attaining them – you are so much more.

When you discover your unique offering as a coach and can accept it, even with the shadows, the badges will lose their power. Interestingly, I have seen and talked to lots of people lately who have the badge of Master Coach and are deciding to let it lapse. Quite apart from the title of 'master' being problematic, the whole concept of making it to the pinnacle is distasteful. The profession is still growing and learning, and so are we as individual coaches. I know that now, over 20 years since I started coaching, the only thing I can be sure of is that I feel there is so much I don't know and can still learn. But that's what keeps it interesting.

You have taken your first tentative step into the second-half-of-coaching life. Be brave, go further and prepare yourself to become a future elder of the profession. Have the courage to accept you can be a wonderful coach as well as being a mediocre one, that you can know lots and nothing at all. and that sometimes you will definitely be a reflection of the criticism you fear, but that just makes you a human coach. I know one thing that ate my confidence when I first started coaching was feeling a fraud because my life was not all sorted. I hadn't fought my dragons. It was only as I reflected on the alternative that I realized the last thing I would want is a perfect coach to witness my vulnerability.

The most precious gift you can bring to your clients, the coaching profession and the world is you, just as you are.

It doesn't matter if you only know the chorus, sing it in your best outside voice. If we are honest with ourselves, we all have work we still need to do, dragons we still need to conquer. In fact, why don't we all stop fighting the dragons, accept them, saddle them up and fly high on them.

Final reflection prompts

- As you consider your reflections across this book, what is your freshest thinking about who you are as a coach?

- What is the unique gift you bring the profession and your clients?

- What are your three priorities for further development in the next 12 months?

Nothing to defend

With nothing to defend
I can listen in wonder
To the whisper of wisdom as she breathes into my heart
Surrender
Let go
All is

Follow on the wisps of silk wings
To the meadow of dreams
Where poppies bring light
To our patchwork of gifts, tied together with
gilt and redemption

Come, tell me your tales
Of dragons and knights
Defending your honour
In chivalrous fights
Created from fear that binds to our darkness
Telling us what we should be

If no darkness exists
Past the mists of our minds
What could we know in wisdoms soft glow
That could loosen those chains from our dreams?

Come spread your cloak
By the fire of your folk
Welcome the ogres and trolls

Let the fables they weave
Uncoil the snake
To a beautiful necklace of pearls

Do these stories they tell
Awaken your spell?
Can you soften and stance and welcome
The stories of old, constants retold
Built on madness, offence and defence
All nothing more than a dandelion clock
To blow to the winds of time

In this meadow of dreams
In the warmth of the fire
Sitting on battlements rubble
Can I open my heart to past enemies, friends?
On our mutual quest to belong

Do we know who we are
Where we came from and go?
Fearless what emerges to light
If the gateway is opened with love

No structure to squeeze us
No rigid conformity
Just the wild freedom of stars to embrace us

Karen Foy

References

Adams, M. (2024) *The Myth of the Untroubled Therapist, Private Life, Professional Practice*, 2nd Edition, Abingdon: Routledge.

Austen, J. (1814) *Mansfield Park. Complete Masterpiece, Genuine Text from the 1814 Edition*, Amazon.

Bachkirova, T. (2015) From competencies to capabilities in the assessment and accreditation of coaches, *International Journal of Evidence Based Coaching and Mentoring*, 13(2), 123–40.

Barrett, L. (2023) *A Jungian Approach to Coaching*, Abingdon: Routledge.

Berne, E. (2010) *Games People Play: The Psychology of Human Relation*, London: Penguin.

Blakey, J. and Day, I. (2012) *Challenging Coaching: Going Beyond Traditional Coaching to Face the FACTS*, London: Nicholas Brealey Publishing.

Brown, B. (2021) *Atlas of the Heart: Mapping Meaningful Connection and the Language of Human Experience*, London: Vermillion.

Carkhuff, R.R. (1969) *Helping and Human Relations Volume 1: Practice and Research*, New York: Holt, Rinehart and Winston.

Carroll, M. and Shaw, E. (2013) *Ethical Maturity in the Helping Professions: Making Difficult Life and Work Decisions*, London: Jessica Kingsley.

Chödrön, P. (2001) *The Places that Scare You: A Guide to Fearlessness*, London: Harper Collins.

Chödrön, P. (2008) *The Pocket Pema Chodron*, Boston, MA: Shambhala.

Clynes, M. (1977) *Sentics: The Touch of Emotions*, Bridport: Prism Press.

De Haan, E., Culpin, V. and Curd, J. (2011) Executive coaching practice: what determines helpfulness for coaching clients, *Personnel Review*, 40(1), 24–44.

Drake, D. (2011) What do coaches need to know? Using the mastery window to assess and develop expertise, *Coaching: An International Journal of Theory, Research and Practice*, 4(2), 138–55.

Garvey, B. (2011) *A Very Short, Fairly Interesting and Reasonably Cheap Book about Coaching and Mentoring*, London: Sage.

Garvey, B. and Stokes, P. (2022) *Coaching & Mentoring: Theory and Practice*, 4th Edition, London: Sage.

Gilbert, E. (2015) *Big Magic: Creative Living Beyond Fear*, London: Bloomsbury.

Hawkins, P. and Smith, N. (2013) *Coaching, Mentoring and Organisational Consultancy: Supervision, Skills & Development*, 2nd Edition, Maidenhead: Open University Press.

Hawkins, P. and Turner, E. (2017) The rise of coaching supervision 2006–2014, *Coaching: An International Journal of Theory, Research and Practice*, 10(2), 102–14.

Heron, J. (1975) *Six Category Intervention Analysis (Human Potential Research Project)*, Guildford: University of Surrey.

Hill, S. (2023) *Where Did You Learn to Behave Like that? A Coaching Guide*, 2nd Edition, Kindle Direct Publishing.

Jones, R.J. (2021) *Coaching with Research in Mind*, Routledge, London.

Loftus, E.F. and Palmer, J.C. (1974) Reconstruction of automobile destruction: an example of the interaction between language and memory, *Journal of Verbal Learning and Verbal Behavior*, 13(5), 585–9.

McKenna, D. and Davis, S. (2009) Hidden in plain sight, *Industrial & Organizational Psychology*, 2(3), 244–60.

Nouwen, H.J.M. (2006) *Bread for the Journey: A Daybook of Wisdom and Faith*, San Francisco, CA: HarperOne.

O'Hanlon, B. (2019) *Do One Thing Different: Ten Simple Ways to Change Your Life*, 20th Anniversary Edition, New York: William Morrow.

Peters, S. (2020) *The Chimp Paradox: The Mind Management Programme to Achieve Success Confidence and Happiness*, London: Vermillion.

Roche, C. and Passmore, J. (2021) *Racial Justice, Equity and Belonging in Coaching*, Henley-on-Thames: Henley Centre for Coaching.

Rogers, C. (1957) The necessary and sufficient conditions of therapeutic personality change, *Journal of Consulting Psychology*, 21, 95–103.

Rohr, R. (2012) *Falling Upward: A Spirituality for the Two Halves of Life*, San Francisco, CA: Jossey-Bass.

Sandler, C. (2011) *Executive Coaching: A Psychodynamic Approach*, Maidenhead: Open University Press.

Scharmer, C.O. (2008) Uncovering the blind spot of leadership, *Leader to Leader*, 2008(47), 52–9.

Shabi, A. (2023) *The Enemies of Coaching*, Aboodi Shabi and Company Ltd. Available at: https://cdn.ymaws.com/association forcoaching.site-ym.com/resource/resmgr/Articles_&_ Handy_Guides/Coaches/Articles/Enemies_of_Coaching.pdf

Silsbee, D. (2008) *Presence-Based Coaching: Cultivating Self-Generating Leaders Through Mind, Body and Heart*, San Francisco, CA: Jossey-Bass.

Smith, W.-A., Passmore, J., Turner, E., Lai, Y-I. and Clutterbuck, D. (2023) *The Ethical Coaches' Handbook: A Guide to Developing Ethical Maturity in Practice*, Abingdon: Routledge.

Steinem, G. (2019) *The Truth Will Set You Free, But First It Will Piss You Off! Thoughts on Life, Love and Rebellion*, Sydney/ London: Murdoch Books.

Sussman, M. (2007) *A Curious Calling*, Lanham, MD: Aronson.

Waitzkin, J. (2007) *The Art of Learning: An Inner Journey to Optimal Performance*, New York: Simon & Schuster.

Whitmore, J. (2009) *Coaching for Performance. GROWing Human Potential and Purpose*, 4th Edition, London: Nicholas Brealey Publishing.

Whyte, D. (2022) *Still Possible*, Langley, WA: Many Rivers Press.

About the author

Karen Foy is a Master Certified Coach with over 20 years' experience. She is a certified coach mentor, supervisor and educator. Karen holds a BA in Psychology from the University of Sheffield and an MSc in Coaching Psychology from the University of East London. She has recently retired as the Programme Director of accredited coaching programmes at Henley Business School, where she is still a visiting tutor and Honorary Fellow. Karen is the founder of The Coach Tribe, an online membership platform where coaches can meet, learn and grow together. Learn more about Karen and The Coach Tribe at www.thecoachtribe.com.

Index

Page numbers in **bold** refer to tables.

accountability 134–35; *see also* goal setting
Adams, Marie 15–16
adding value: confidence in coaching 34; the myth of the objective observer 46–47; reasons to coach 18–25
ADHD, as a coach 61, 69–70, 107, 146
'aha' moments 16, 23, 122
Alexander, Graham 85
Andrews, Holly 10
anger, as sentic state 32, 33
archetypes 42, **43–4**
artificial intelligence (AI): impact on coaching profession 9–11; interpreting mental states 105–7; transactional coaching of performance 86
assumptions, made by everyone 74–6
awareness *see* self-awareness
awe, as sentic state 32

Barrett, Laurence 39
Berne, Eric 44–5
biases 74–6
biometrics 105–7
birdwatching metaphor 67–71
boat metaphor 19, 102
boundaries in coaching 17–18
'brave' space 31–2, 33
breaking the rules *see* rules, and breaking them

Brown, Brené 105
Brown, Paul 73–4

caregiving, reasons to coach 16
Carkhuff, Robert 110–11, **111**, 124–5
Carroll, M. 140–1, 142, 143
chimp brain 101–2
Chödrön, Pema 35, 42
clarity in conversation 115
co-creation 81–4, 125
co-pilot 102
coach-client relationship: asking a client about themselves 73–4; birdwatching metaphor 67–71; goal setting 89–95; interrupting a client 91–2; the objective observer 40–6; transference 41; translating from therapeutic relationship 29–30; unconditional positive regard 30
coaching alliance 59–64
coaching competency perspective 21
coaching effectiveness: confrontative style for leaders 116; major factors 23–4; power of listening 106; *see also* competency frameworks
coaching, exploring your personal agenda in becoming a coach 15–25

coaching mindset: goal
setting 85–95; how to
develop 21–5; reflection
and supervision 51; and
self-awareness 49–54
colour blindness 75
competency frameworks 82–3,
121–6; *see also* coaching
effectiveness
concreteness 115, 133–4
confidence in coaching 34–5
confrontation 116
'the confession' 87
contract, between client and
coach 89
counter-transference 41
curiosity 67–71, 76

'dancing in the moment' 97–102
Davis, S, 23–4, 133
disengagement, of a client
135, 136–7

effectiveness *see* coaching
effectiveness; competency
frameworks
emotions: AI interpreting mental
states 105–7; fearing
opening emotions 101–2;
sentic states 31–4
empathy 32–3, 114–15
'empty boat' 19, 102
endings, with a particular client
135, 136–7
energy, sentic states 31–4
eros, as sentic state 32
ethical maturity 139–43
executive coaching 12

'the fall' 9–14
feedback, fears about 20–1
first half of life teaching 8–9;
elders of the coaching

profession 147; empty
boat metaphor 112;
presence 27; transcending
the rules 81–4; trusting the
process 35–6

genuineness 114–15
goal setting 85–95; fearing
running out of time 99–
100; flexible approach to
129–37; noticing insights
and change 98–9; the
original outcome 98
golden thread metaphor 90
grief, as sentic state 32, 33
GROW (goal, realities, options,
way forward) model
85–6
guide-rails 146

halves of life 8–9; elders
of the coaching
profession 147; empty
boat metaphor 19, 112;
presence 27; transcending
the rules 81–4
hatred, as sentic state 32
Hawkins Peter 32
Heron, John 116
Hill, Sarah 42, 71
hope (as client belief) 24
humanity of coaching 11

immediacy 116–17
'in the moment' listening 116–17
innate wisdom 52
International Coaching
Federation 121–2
interrupting a client 91–2

Jones, Rebecca 30–1
joy, as sentic state 32
Jung, Carl 8–9, 39, 87

LGBTQIA2S+ community 75
listening, and awareness 124–5
listening, four levels of 109
listening with purpose 109–19,
        133–4
love, as sentic state 32, 33
love-hate relationship 82

McKenna, D. 23–4, 133
maturity, professional and
        ethical 139–43

mentoring, relationship to
        coaching 70–1
mindset: goal setting 85–95; how
        to develop 21–5; reflection
        and supervision 51; and
        self-awareness 49–54

Neill, Michael 52, 125
neurodivergence 69–70
nonverbal language 105–7
Nothing to Defend 149–50
Nouwen, Henri 110

the objective observer: coach-
        client relationship 40–6;
        discharging the loyal
        soldier 46–7; as myth 39–40
online coaching 145

Passmore, J. 75
peer supervision 141
performance: and artificial
        intelligence 86; external
        standards and internal
        drivers 27–9; and presence
        27, 29–31, 34–5; sentic
        states 31–4; training and
        transcending the rules 82–3;
        'trust the process' 35–7
personal agenda, reasons to
        coach 15–25

personal relations *see* coach-client
        relationship
Peters, Steve 53, 101
placebo effect 106
Portkey metaphor 112–13
presence: client conversations
        97–102; how to
        increase 34–5; and
        performance 27, 29–31;
        and self-awareness 49–54
procrastination 69
professional maturity 139–43
PROMISES mnemonic **59–60**
psychopathy 10

questions, how to ask 121–6

race, and colour blindness 75
reflection: ethical and professional
        maturity 142–3; flexible
        approach to goals 129–37;
        and silence 117–19; and
        supervision 49, 50–1; *see
        also* self-reflection
rejection, fear of 45
relationships *see* coach-client
        relationship
resilience 86
responsibilities, as a coach
        17–18
Roche, C. 75
Rogers, Carl 16, 29–30, 110–11
Rohr, Richard 8–9, 46
rules, and breaking them 7–8;
        change over time 145–8;
        ethical and professional
        maturity 139–43;
        fear of leading the
        client 100–1; fearing
        opening emotions 101–2;
        the objective observer 40;
        transcending the rules
        36, 62–3

Scharmer, Otto 109
second half of life teaching:
    elders of the coaching
    profession 147; empty
    boat metaphor 19, 112;
    level of responsibility 23;
    presence 27; transcending
    the rules 9, 81–4; trusting
    the process 35–6
self-awareness: asking
    questions 124–5;
    elevator pitch 63; how to
    increase 36–7; presence
    and mindset 49–54;
    reasons to coach 15;
    trust 13
self-discovery 5, 50
self-reflection 12
sentic states 31–4
sex, and bias 75
Shabi, Aboodi 27, 73
Shaw, E. 140–1, 142, 143
Shohet, Robin 19
shortcuts 7–8
silence 117–19
SMART (specific, measurable,
    achievable, relevant and
    time-bound) goals 129
social niceties 91–2
soldier metaphor 46–7
Steinem, Gloria 12
stereotypes 74–6
supervision: empty boat
    metaphor 19; ending
    sessions with a particular
    client 136–7; ethical and
    professional maturity 141–
    2; goal setting 94–5; by

peers 141; and reflection
    49, 50–1; unconditional
    positive regard 30

technological change see artificial
    intelligence (AI); online
    coaching
therapeutic relationship,
    conditions for 29–30;
    see also coach-client
    relationship
therapist training 15–16
timings, coaching sessions 132–3
to-do list 107, 129
tools and techniques, effectiveness
    of 23–4
transactional analysis 44–5
transactional coaching 86
transcending the rules 36, 81–4;
    coaching alliance 62–3;
    ethical and professional
    maturity 142–3; fear of
    leading the client 100–1;
    interrupting 91–2; task and
    person 105–6
transference 41
'trust the process' 35–7

unconditional positive regard 30

warrior in training mindset 35
well-being 86, 105
whistle-calls 124
Whitmore, John, Sir 85
Whyte, David 51, 53, 86
working agreement, client
    conversations 97–102
writing this book 3–5